THE COMPLETE BOOK OF
KNOTS & ROPEWORK

OVER 200 TECHNIQUES WITH STEP-BY-STEP PHOTOGRAPHS

GEOFFREY BUDWORTH

LORENZ BOOKS

This edition is published by Lorenz Books, an imprint of Anness Publishing Ltd
Hermes House, 88–89 Blackfriars Road, London SE1 8HA; tel. 020 7401 2077; fax 020 7633 9499

www.lorenzbooks.com; www.annesspublishing.com

If you like the images in this book and would like to investigate using them for publishing, promotions or advertising,
please visit our website www.practicalpictures.com for more information.

UK agent: The Manning Partnership Ltd; tel. 01225 478444; fax 01225 478440; sales@manning-partnership.co.uk

UK distributor: Grantham Book Services Ltd; tel. 01476 541080; fax 01476 541061; orders@gbs.tbs-ltd.co.uk

North American agent/distributor: National Book Network; tel. 301 459 3366; fax 301 429 5746; www.nbnbooks.com

Australian agent/distributor: Pan Macmillan Australia; tel. 1300 135 113; fax 1300 135 103; customer.service@macmillan.com.au

New Zealand agent/distributor: David Bateman Ltd; tel. (09) 415 7664; fax (09) 415 8892

Publisher: Joanna Lorenz
Project Editor: Sarah Duffin
Designer: Michael Morey
Photographer: Rodney Forte
Editorial Reader: Joy Wotton
Production Controller: Julie Hadingham

Previously published as *The Ultimate Encyclopedia of Knots and Ropework*

ETHICAL TRADING POLICY

At Anness Publishing we believe that business should be conducted in an ethical and ecologically sustainable way, with respect for the
environment and a proper regard to the replacement of the natural resources we employ.

As a publisher, we use a lot of wood pulp to make high-quality paper for printing, and that wood commonly comes from spruce trees.
We are therefore currently growing more than 500,000 trees in two Scottish forest plantations near Aberdeen – Berrymoss
(130 hectares/320 acres) and West Touxhill (125 hectares/305 acres). The forests we manage contain twice the number of trees employed
each year in paper-making for our books.

Because of this ongoing ecological investment programme, you, as our customer, can have the pleasure and reassurance of knowing that a tree
is being cultivated on your behalf to naturally replace the materials used to make the book you are holding.

Our forestry programme is run in accordance with the UK Woodland Assurance Scheme (UKWAS) and will be certified by the
internationally recognized Forest Stewardship Council (FSC). The FSC is a non-government organization dedicated to promoting
responsible management of the world's forests. Certification ensures forests are managed in an environmentally sustainable and socially
responsible basis. For further information about this scheme, go to www.annesspublishing.com/trees

CAUTION

Do not use any of the knots, bends, hitches etc in this book for a purpose that involves foreseeable risk of loss, damage or injury without the
appropriate training and equipment. Cavers, climbers, rescue workers, wilderness or ocean-going adventurers who wish to use a particular
knot for those (or any other) activities and pursuits are strongly advised to seek the advice of qualified practitioners first. This book is
intended only to be a safe and simple introduction to knot tying.

Contents

INTRODUCTION

"It is extraordinary how little the average individual knows about the art of making even the simplest knots."

(R.M. ABRAHAM – *WINTER NIGHTS' ENTERTAINMENTS*, 1932)

Knotting is an enjoyable pastime. Most people can learn to tie knots and soon acquire an impressive repertoire. Knot tying is as absorbing as reading a good book, and the end product is as satisfactory as a completed crossword or jigsaw puzzle – but with many more practical applications. Everyone ought to know a few knots; that is why the International Guild of Knot Tyers (IGKT), founded in 1982, is now a recognized educational charity. Nobody should be over-dependent upon safety pins and superglues, patent zips (zippers) and clips and other fastenings, when a suitable length of cord and the right combination of knots are cheaper, consume less of the planet's scarce energy resources and often work better.

There are several thousand individual knots and an almost infinite number of variations of some of them. In addition, new knots emerge every year from the fingers of innovative knot tyers to increase the existing numbers. Then there are the ornamental aspects: macramé; leather-braiding and whipmaking; Chinese decorative knotting; Japanese *kumihimo* and other elaborate braiding or plaiting techniques; traditional British corn dollies; tassels, tatting and crocheting. Magicians and escapologists practise knot and rope trickery. Mathematicians venture into three dimensions when they explore the abstruse topological field of knot theory. For periodic dabblers and serious devotees alike, knotting is a delightful pursuit, a lifelong obsession, and for a few fortunate individuals it is a wonderful way to make a living. This book cannot possibly cover everything outlined above, but the 200 or so carefully chosen knots it contains will gently challenge those new to knot tying and, it is hoped, even teach more experienced hands a thing or two.

KEY TO KNOT USER GROUPS

Angling/Fishing

Boating/Sailing

Caving/Climbing

General Purpose

Outdoor Pursuits

History, Origins and Uses

Cave dwellers tied knots. The 1960s American knotting writer, Cyrus Lawrence Day, believed that knots pre-dated (perhaps by several millenia) the time when humankind learned to use fire and cultivate the soil, invented the wheel and harnessed the wind. Unfortunately, any tangible evidence for this has long ago decomposed, but the first knotted materials are likely to have been vines, sinews and raw-hide strips from animal carcasses. There are some credible clues from non-perishable artefacts dug up by archaeologists that humans used knots and cordage more than 300,000 years ago. However, there is nothing to indicate what knots were employed before the earliest surviving specimens, less than 10,000 years old – fragments of nets, fishing lines, amulets and clothes – found in prehistoric garbage dumps and with mummified bog bodies. So we know that Neolithic folk tied the overhand knot and half hitch, reef

✦ ABOVE
The artful geometry of rope.

✦ BELOW
Codline and water-resistant coir contrast with darkly tarred and weatherproofed, aromatic hemp hawsers and spun yarn.

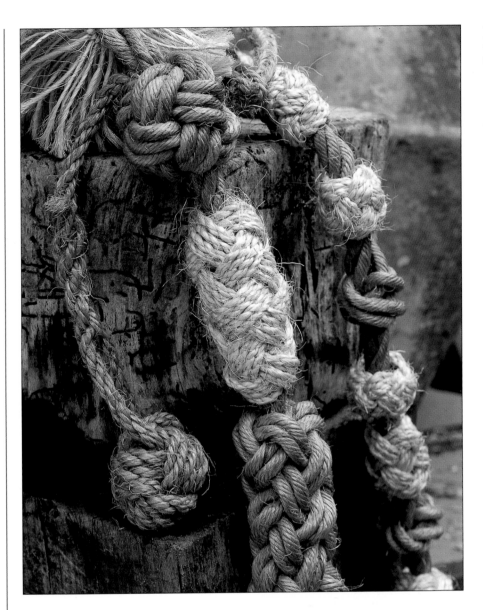

♦ LEFT
Practical and decorative marlinespike
seamanship.

the time human history was first
recorded, the artful geometry of
rope was already established,
inherited from a prehistoric time
beyond the memories of the
oldest and wisest scribes.

KNOT LORE
Knotted cords were used in
primitive cultures to keep track of
dates, events and genealogies; to
recount folk lore and legends; as
mnemonic memory cues in prayer
or confession, and to record
trading transactions and
inventories. Both the rosary and
the abacus probably evolved from
knotted cords. The Incas of
ancient Peru made ropes of
maguey, derived from the
tropical agave plants, that were

♦ BELOW
Old glass fishing floats are protected by
a network of meshes.

(square) knot, clove hitch and a
running noose – and probably
others too. They used them to
snare animals, catch fish, tote
loads, perhaps as surgical slings –
and to strangle the occasional
enemy or sacrificial offering. The
Late Stone Age lake-dwellers of
Switzerland were excellent
ropemakers and weavers, who
also used the mesh knot (similar
to a sheet bend) in their nets, and
they would have instantly
recognized the cord reticules that
secure and protect those glass
floats – now found in many
waterside cafes – which once
supported the gill or drift nets of
seagoing fishing fleets. Indeed, by

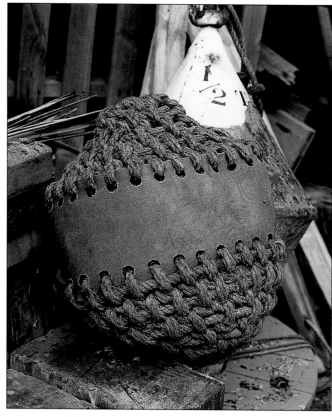

strong enough for the primitive suspension bridges they constructed over mountain chasms. They also produced excellent textiles, and their bureaucracy, lacking a written language, relied upon elaborate coloured and knotted fringes of cord known as *quipus* (Quechua: *quipu* = knot) to keep decimalized records and so administer an empire that extended 4,827 km (3,000 miles) from north to south.

In Hawaii, as recently as 1822, illiterate tax gatherers kept a comprehensive tally of what was collected from each and every inhabitant on the island, in cash or kind, by means of a cord over 800 metres (half a mile) long, to which were attached knots of various colours and materials – one representing dollars, another hogs, others indicating dogs, pieces of sandalwood, and so on.

Ancient Egyptian art tells us regrettably little about their knots, but we know that they applied the theorem of the Greek mathematician Pythagoras (*c.* 580–500 BC) to solve practical surveying and building problems by making 12 equal knotted intervals in a rope and then stretching it into a 3,4,5 triangle.

Even the legendary Gordian knot of ancient Greece is a

♦ ABOVE LEFT
A "pudding" fender.

♦ ABOVE RIGHT
A boat fender neatly enhanced with a cast-off length of machinery drive-belt in the centre.

♦ LEFT
Needle-hitched bottles or flasks, with a rigger's canvas tool bucket and a kitbag.

♦ OPPOSITE
A sailor's ornate chest becket or handle.

◆ RIGHT
Whisk brushes, in progress and completed.

mystery. Gordius, father of Midas, was a peasant who rose to be king of Phrygia and – so the story goes – tied his by then redundant farm cart with leather harness traces and presented it to the temple of Zeus. So intricate was the knot that nobody could untie it, and the oracles proclaimed that whoever did so was destined to become emperor of all Asia. Alexander the Great tried his hand at this knotted puzzle but soon lost patience and, according to one account, severed it with his sword. "To cut the Gordian knot" came to mean disposing of any intractable problem at a stroke.

SAILORS AND COWBOYS

It is not necessary to like boats to enjoy knot tying. Indeed boating these days yields few opportunities to tie knots. It is equally wrong to assume that knot tying emerged only from sailing-ship crews. It is true that it flourished when

ropework evolved aboard the massive square-rigged warships and merchantmen of the 18th and 19th centuries when sailors had to cope with increasingly complex rigging. The sailor's chest becket or handle shows how seamen then turned in their leisure hours from practical to ornamental knotwork. This era lasted, however, for barely 150 years. Cowboys tied fancy knots and braids every bit as elaborate as those done by sailormen. Ashore,

knots had always been tools for those who engaged in particular trades and pursuits: archers and anglers, basketmakers, bellringers, bookbinders, builders and butchers, carters, cobblers and cowboys, dockers (longshoremen), falconers, farmers, firemen and fishermen, gunners, jewellers, millers, pedlars and poachers, riggers (in circus and theatre), shopkeepers, soldiers, steeplejacks, stevedores and surgeons, waggoners and weavers. There

◆ BOTTOM
Cargo-handling hooks for dockers
(longshoremen) – or prostheses for
disabled pirates.

◆ BELOW
A monkey's fist door-stop.

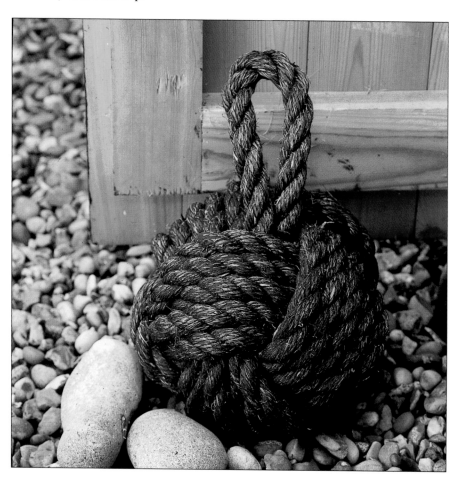

was a time when a handy whisk
(brush) and maybe a chunky
door-stop, both made from rope,
could be found in many homes.

MYSTICS AND MEDICS

The practice of knotting is an
ancient one. Knots were believed
by some to possess supernatural
properties and wizards and
witches were known to have
traded upon that fact. The
legendary Greek epic poet Homer
(traditionally a blind minstrel
living in the 8th century BC)
has Aeolus, king of the winds,
give Odysseus a leather bag in
which all of the winds are tied up.

The Greek philosopher Plato
(c. 428–347 BC) detested the
blacker aspects of knot magic and
wrote, in his *Laws*, that those
who preyed upon the gullible by

means of knot sorcery should be
put to death. As recently as 1718,
the Bordeaux parliament in
France sentenced someone to be
burnt alive for bewitching
an entire family by means of
magic knots.

In his *Natural History*, the
Roman scientist and historian
Pliny the Elder (AD 23–79)
advised that wounds bound with
a Hercules knot (a reef or square
knot) healed more quickly.
Indeed, those who learn first aid
today still use this knot for slings
and bandages but are unaware of
the reason why.

Preserved in the medical
collections of the 4th century AD
Greek physician Oreibasius of

◆ BELOW
Antique hardwood fids, used to help tuck in the working ends of a knot.

◆ BELOW
Classic boat fenders of coir.

Pergamum are 18 knots, originally described three centuries earlier by Heraklas as surgeons' knots. These are regrettably not illustrated, but have been interpreted to include the overhand knot, reef (square) knot, the clove hitch, a noose, a fisherman's loop knot, the jug, jar or bottle sling, Tom Fool's knot, a cat's cradle, the true lover's knot, and – quite possibly – the constrictor knot.

An early Scandinavian form of birth control, when a couple decided they had a large enough family, was to name the last-born boy Knut (meaning "knot"). In some places it was thought that a cure for warts was to tie knots in a piece of string, one knot for each wart, and then to discard the string; thereafter, the first person to contact the string would acquire the warts.

One of the earliest heraldic knots was the carrick bend used by the Saxon leader Hereward the Wake, who in 1071 AD revolted against William the Conqueror. In heraldry, it is still called the Wake knot.

Romantic allusions to the true lover's knot continually crop up in English literature after 1495 AD. Although there is no clue as to whether such a knot existed, several contemporary knots, with two interlocking identical parts, are referred to by that name.

CLASSIC KNOTS
Who invented or discovered all of these classic knots? Some of the simpler ones must have arisen spontaneously, in separate regions of the world, wherever somebody picked up a flexible bit of material and idly toyed with it. Then again, others are likely to have been spread by foreign traders and occupying armies. Imagine tracing a particular knot – say the distinctive jug, jar or bottle sling – from hand to hand and back through the centuries to its originator (an impossible notion, of course). History, as far as the activity of people was concerned, might have to be revised and rewritten.

Materials

Rope has been made by man since the Stone Age, utilising the materials that were available. European hunter-gatherers, 10,000 years ago, grew only one crop – flax – and that was for rope, not food; the ancient Egyptians and Persians made rope from papyrus and flax. Even a captive orang-utan is reported to have made a kind of rope from its bedding material and then swung from it.

It is no surprise that man has gone to such lengths to develop and enhance rope-making materials. Rope enabled humankind to probe the deepest caves and to seek fuel and ores in underground mines; to migrate over rugged terrain with pack animals; to capture, harness and ride other beasts; to sail and cross oceans in search of treasure, trade, conquest and colonization. Rope concentrated the efforts of the labour force that built the great Egyptian pyramids and created the blocks and tackles with which medieval European stone masons erected their Gothic cathedrals and castles.

VEGETABLE FIBRE CORDAGE

As we have seen, until this century, rope was made from the shredded, combed and graded fibres of plant stems such as flax and jute, or from the leaves of sisal and abaca (hemp). It was made from fibres attached to seeds (cotton), and from other vegetable materials as diverse as fibrous coconut shells (coir),

NATURAL ROPE

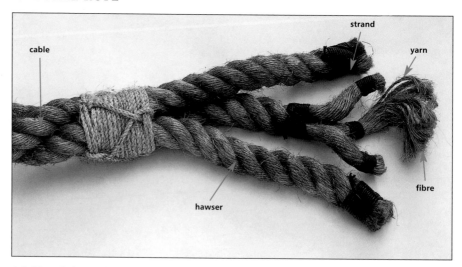

A lefthanded (or S-laid) cable consists of three righthanded (Z-laid) hawsers. Each of these ropes has three lefthanded (counterclockwise) strands made from numerous righthanded (clockwise) yarns, spun from vegetable fibres.

horse and camel (even human) hair, date palms, reeds, esparto grass, wool and silk.

Because of its origins in nature, such cordage is also referred to as natural fibre. These fibres were spun clockwise (or righthanded) to create long yarns. Several of these yarns were next twisted up anticlockwise (counterclockwise) into strands. Finally, three strands were laid up clockwise or righthanded which created a typical rope.

The incurably romantic – who wish that square-rigged sailing ships were still commonplace – regret the demise of these vegetable fibre ropes, with their evocative smells and every shade of gold and brown; but, with the emergence of synthetic (manmade) cordage, the shortcomings of natural fibre ropes became intolerable. They were comparatively weak, even when scaled up to enormous diameters. Unable to withstand

SYNTHETIC (MANMADE) ROPE

A 14 mm (7/12 in) diameter, soft matt polyester, 16-plait sheath encloses a hawser-laid core of several thousand high-tenacity polyester filaments.

Vegetable fibre knotted cordage in its
natural element.

Natural fibre ropes vary in colour and
may be blonde or brunette.

much abrasion, vegetable fibre
cordage was also prey to mildew,
rot, insects and vermin. It swelled
when wet (so knots became
impossible to untie) and froze in
icy conditions with irreparable
weakening as brittle fibres broke.
Such ropes were also rough on
the hands.

Obtainable only from
specialized sources, and at a
premium price, the use of natural
fibre cordage is now very limited,
– except in situations (such as
filming a costume drama, rigging
a classic wooden boat, and
designing the interior decor and
window dressing of nautical pubs,
clubs and restaurants) where the
appearance of an earlier period
must be evoked. Some thoughtful

souls, however, concerned by
what they perceive to be a
profligate use of the earth's finite
resources, prophesy an eventual
return to natural fibre cordage,
the raw materials of which can be
harvested from renewable growing crops, without destructive
ecological footprints.

Sisal rope is still sold for
general purposes. Children shin
up best-quality soft hemp ropes in
school gyms. Coir is used for boat
fenders. And for weather-resistant
serving and seizing of wire and
rope rigging by professional
riggers, balls of tarred hemp spun
yarn are still sold in several sizes.

It used to be that a rope could
only be as long as the ropewalk
(open field or long shed) where it

was made – although, of course,
two or more could then be
spliced together – but compact
modern machinery has overcome
this and, with extruded synthetic
filaments, rope of practically any
length can be made.

SYNTHETIC (MANMADE) CORDAGE

Discovered and developed by
research chemists in the 1930s,
the basic elements for synthetic
cordage are: very fine continuous
clusters of multifilaments, less
than 50 microns/$\frac{1}{500}$ in across and
of uniform diameter and circular
cross-section; coarser monofilaments, individually more than 50
microns/$\frac{1}{500}$ in in diameter;
discontinuous staple fibres (from

◆ LEFT
Sisal fibres are rough and hairy, but soft to the touch.

◆ BELOW
Cordage lengths are no longer limited by the extent of the ropewalk, either field or long shed, where it was made.

Terylene and Dacron); polypropylene, which is best for mundane domestic use; polyethylene (or Polythene), often sold as balls of twine; and a few so-called "miracle fibres" (such as Kevlar, Dyneema or Spectra) representing the latest and more expensive cutting edge of ropemaking technology. There are two grades of nylon: Nylon 66, discovered in the Du Pont laboratories, was the first manmade fibre of merit available to the cordage industry, and Nylon 6, subsequently developed by I.G. Farbenindustrie. Terylene was a British development from investigations at the Calico Printers Association, the sole rights were then taken up by Imperial Chemical Industries.

2 cm/⅝ in to 2 m/2 yd in length) made by cutting multifilaments or monofilaments into discrete lengths; and flat, narrow, ribbon-like strings produced from extruded split or fibrillated film. The brightly coloured balls of twine often found in hardware shops and stores are usually split film products, as are the larger balls and cops (cylindrical reels) sold at garden centres for horticulture use or as baling twines for agricultural machinery.

All of these raw materials make cordage that is size-for-size stronger and lighter than its vegetable fibre equivalent. A three-strand nylon rope is more than twice as strong as a manila one, yet it weighs half as much and may last four to five times as long. Many can be dyed a variety of colours (even including psychedelic patterns). Almost as strong when wet, they have a high tensile (breaking) strength and are also able to withstand sudden shock loading. Although not

plagued by the ills that afflict natural fibre ropes, they are more susceptible to heat generated by friction – softening, melting and even parting in extreme cases.

The most common manmade materials are: polyamide (nylon), the strongest man-made cordage; polyester (best known trade names

✦ RIGHT
Man-made cordage is smoother than
natural yarn, but stronger.

MANMADE MATERIALS

"MIRACLE FIBRES"

Kevlar – discovered by Du Pont as long ago as 1965 – is an organic polymer immune to moisture and rot. Weight-for-weight it is twice as strong as nylon, but with low elasticity, and it has been used to replace wire halyards. Then there is Spectra or HMPE, the brand name of Allied Chemicals who manufactured this super-lightweight polyethylene (marketed by others as Dyneema and Admiral 2000). Its phenomenal tensile strength is greater than that of stainless steel. Released in 1985, it looks set to supersede Kevlar. The considerable cost of these will not deter ocean yacht racers or climbers, for whom competitive edge and extra safety margins are worth any price, but they are not recommended for routine knot tying.

POLYAMIDE (NYLON)

Polyamide is the strongest manmade cordage (although 10–15 per cent less when wet) and cheaper than polyester. It is very elastic, stretching under a load anything from 10 per cent to 40 per cent, then regaining its original length when the load is removed. This makes it suitable for mooring lines, also towing and rock-climbing ropes – but not in the restricted space of caves or crowded moorings, where stretchy ropes could be a liability. It does not float, so nylon can also be used for yachting anchor warps. The best colour to buy is white, as colouring may weaken the fibres by 10 per cent (while

certainly adding a lot to the price). A fairly high melting point of up to 260°C (478°F) ensures a reduced risk of melting due to friction; but be warned, it will, like all synthetics, soften and be irredeemably weakened at a much lower temperature than its melting point. Polyamide withstands attack from alkalis (and acids, to a lesser degree), oils and organic solvents. It has acceptable resistance to photochemical degradation from the ultra-violet wavelengths in sunlight, and to abrasion. Domestic consumers of this product will be impressed to learn that it is recommended for deep-sea towing and widely used in the off-shore oil industry.

POLYESTER (TERYLENE, DACRON)

Three-quarters the strength of nylon (but equally strong wet or dry), polyester does not stretch half as much, and pre-stretching during manufacture can remove most of the latent elasticity it does possess. Consequently it is recommended for standing rigging, sheets and halyards, where stretch is unwanted but high tensile strength is required, even replacing wire. It resists acids (and alkalis, to a lesser extent), oils and organic solvents. Like nylon, it does not float and it has about the same melting point and resistance to sunlight – but polyester wears better.

POLYETHYLENE (POLYTHENE)

Cheap, light (but it barely floats in water), without much stretch,

polyethylene is fairly hard-wearing and durable but has the lowest melting point of the four "poly" materials. It is sold in hardware stores as balls of twine and is used in the fishing industry, but it is too stiff and springy for most knot tying.

POLYPROPYLENE

In terms of cost and performance, this cordage may be ranked between vegetable fibre and the superior (nylon, terylene) manmade fibre cordage. Made from multifilament, monofilament, staple fibre or split film, it is the most versatile of synthetic fibres. Large quantities are manufactured and sold, at reasonable prices, via hardware and DIY shops and stores for all kinds of mundane work entailing no high performance risks. It has one-third to half the breaking strength of nylon and a much lower melting point – around 150°C (302°F) – rendering it useless for any task where friction generates anything approaching that amount of heat, but, as it is the lightest of the synthetics, and floats indefinitely, it is the obvious choice for lifelines and water-skiing towlines. It is completely rot-proof and resistant to most acids, alkalis and oils, but affected adversely by bleaching agents and some industrial solvents, while some cheaper brands denature in bright sun. For lovers of traditional cordage, there is a light brown rope – reliable, hardwearing and inexpensive – made from polypropylene to resemble hemp.

Types of Rope

Vegetable fibres are short and must be spun and twisted to create the long yarns and strands needed for rope. It is the countless fibre ends that give traditional ropes their characteristic hairy appearance and useful surface grip. Long synthetic filaments run the full length of the ropes they form, so manmade cordage is smooth – unless the filaments are purposely chopped into shorter lengths of staple fibres to make ropes that recapture the desirable handling qualities of the older natural cordage. More fibres and yarns make thicker cordage, and a rope that is twice the diameter of another will, as a general rule, be four times as strong (because the cross-sectional area has been quadrupled).

LAID

It is the twist and counter-twist imparted during manufacture that holds rope strands together and gives them their geometry,

strength and flexibility. If very little tension is applied during the ropemaking process, the product will be floppy and flexible (soft laid), whereas great tension produces stiff (hard laid) stuff. Hard laid lines wear better but soft laid ones are preferable for tying knots. A three-strand rope is known as a hawser (and so is hawser-laid). Three hawsers laid up lefthanded make a nine-strand cable. Four-strand (shroud-laid) rope is less common and requires a core of yarns to fill the hollow space that inevitably occurs at the heart of such ropes. Lefthanded hawsers (and righthanded cables) are rare but not unknown. Textile workers, weavers and braiders prefer the terms S-laid (lefthanded) and Z-laid (righthanded) for the alternating twist and countertwist of yarns, strands and ropes.

BRAIDED

Braided vegetable fibre cordage has always been rare, except in

small sizes for flag halyards and sash window cord. In synthetics it is commonplace and in many ways preferable to strands. An 8- or 16-plait (braid) is more flexible and stretches less than laid line. It does not kink, nor does it impart a spinning motion when loaded (as laid lines tend to do). Some braided cordage is hollow. In most, however, a separate core provides strength, elasticity and other essential properties, reinforced by the sheath, which adds extra surface characteristics, such as friction, feel, resistance to abrasion, sunlight and chemicals. This core may take several different forms, in which a braided outer sheath encloses heart strands that can be braided, laid or composed of parallel multifilaments, monofilaments or yarns. Braid-on-braid is acknowledged to be the strongest of cordage constructions and braided synthetic lines are the most versatile of all cordage.

PLAITED
Eight or sixteen ropes, usually nylon, are woven in pairs to create mighty mooring warps for supertankers.

SHEATH-AND-CORE
Climbing ropes are a special class of cordage, often referred to by the European designation kernmantel (core-sheath). Static ropes take the full weight of climbers and are designed for the wear, tear and occasional short fall of regular climbing; while dynamic ropes are used for safety, generally unloaded, but with the extra elasticity and integral strength to cope with potentially disastrous falls and uncontrolled spins. Single ropes are manufactured in 11 mm/²⁄₅ in diameters, plus or minus 5 mm/ ¼ in, while half-ropes of 9 mm/ ³⁄₈ in diameter, plus or minus 2 mm/¹⁄₁₂ in, are intended to be used doubled. Climbing ropes should have high melting points

to absorb the heat generated by abseiling (rappelling) and belaying. Obtain specialist advice on the detailed properties of these ropes and look for the UIAA (Union Internationale des Associations d'Alpinisme) label of approval.

Kernmantel accessory cord, used for slings and other attachments, can be obtained in diameters that range from 4–11 mm/¹⁄₆–²⁄₅ in.

Woven nylon webbing comes in widths from 10–75 mm/⁵⁄₁₂–3 in, but the width most commonly seen is 25 mm/1 in. A tubular tape, resembling a flattened hollow tube, handles and knots easily due to its suppleness, but a flat weave, similar to that found in car seat belts, is stronger, stiffer and has better resistance to wear and abrasion. It is highly versatile and not too expensive for harnesses, belts and slings, and it also makes excellent luggage rack lashings (straps) for cars and vans.

KEY TO TYPES OF ROPE	
1	8-strand nylon, 16 mm/²⁄₃ in anchor braid.
2	3-strand nylon, 14 mm/⁷⁄₁₂ in hawser.
3	3-strand polyester, 14 mm/⁷⁄₁₂ in hawser.
4	3-strand spun polyester, 14 mm/⁷⁄₁₂ in hawser (resembling natural fibre rope).
5	3-strand monofilament polypropylene, 14 mm/⁷⁄₁₂ in hawser.
6	3-strand staple/spun polypropylene, 14 mm/⁷⁄₁₂ in hawser.
7	16-plait matt polyester, 14 mm/⁷⁄₁₂ inbraid-on-braid rope, with an unusual core (itself a16-plait enclosing an 8-plait), creating three concentric layers.
8	16-plait matt polyester, 16 mm/²⁄₃ in braid-on-braid rope (with a double layered core, as above).
9	16-plait pre-stretched polyester, 16 mm/²⁄₃ in braid-on-braid (with an 8-plait core) rope.
10	16-plait Dyneema, 12 mm/½ in braid-on-braid rope (with a two-layered core).
11	16-plait Dyneema, 10 mm/ ⁵⁄₁₂ in braid-on-braid rope (with a two-layered core).
12	16-plait polypropylene, 9 mm/ ³⁄₈ in braid-on-braid cord (with a hard-laid 8-plait cord core).
13	16-plait polyester, 6 mm/¼ in sheath-and-core cord (with a heart of four 3-strand strings).
14	8-plait matt polyester, 10 mm/ ⁵⁄₁₂ in braid-on-braid rope (with an 8-plait core).
15	8-plait multifilament polypropylene, 8 mm/¹⁄₃ in braid-on-braid cord (with an 8-plait core).
16	8-plait pre-stretched polyester, 6 mm/¼ in sheath-and-core cord (with a heart of three 3-strand strings).

10   11   12   13   14   15   16

Breaking Strengths

Ropemakers' brochures and leaflets usually contain tables listing the minimum average breaking load of every type and size of their cordage products. Unfortunately, the data differs from company to company, depending upon the tests and equipment each firm uses, making comparisons difficult.

SPECIFICATIONS

Product specifications may blur the facts: for example, a "mooring line", made for specialized markets, may consist of an elastic nylon core inside a hard-wearing polyester sheath, while many mass-produced and comparatively cheap cordage items, sold for the domestic market, can be much weaker. Nevertheless, an appreciation of the main rope and cordage species can be gained from the following outline. The minimum breaking strength of a 4 mm/⅙ in diameter slim nylon cord of 3-strand or 8-plait construction is likely to be around 320 kg/705 lb, which might withstand two 159-kg/25-stone Japanese sumo wrestlers having a tug-of-war. For standard 3-strand polyester of the same diameter the figure is a trifle lower – 295 kg/650 lb – but an 8-plait construction combined with pre-stretch treatment changes that to around 450 kg/990 lb. Polypropylene of the same diameter is variously quoted at 140 kg/309 lb, 250 kg/551 lb and even 430 kg/925 lb; polyethylene is about 185 kg/408 lb, while the average breaking strength of a 4 mm/⅙ in cord of Dyneema/Admiral 2000/Spectra is a remarkable 650 kg/1,432 lb. To achieve these kinds of performance with natural fibres, it would be necessary to have at least a 25 per cent increase in diameter to 5 mm/⅕ in manila or 33.3 per cent to 6 mm/¼ in sisal.

LARGER SIZES

With a 10 mm/$^5\!/_{12}$ in thin nylon 3-strand hawser, the minimum breaking strength increases to around 2,400 kg/5,292 lb. That is almost two-and-a-half metric tonnes, the weight of a large motor vehicle. Again, the average figure is somewhat less for polyester at 2,120 kg/about 2 tons; 1,382 kg/1⅓ tons for polypropylene; and 1,090 kg/just over a ton for polyethelene. Dyneema/Admiral 2000/Spectra, by contrast, would be about 4,000 kg/about 4 tons. The same size of rope in manila could only cope with 710 kg/1,565 lb and sisal with 635 kg/1,400 lb.

Finally, for a sizeable 24 mm/1 in rope diameter, the average quoted breaking strengths are: nylon = 13 tonnes/12.8 tons; polyester = 10 tonnes/9.8 tons; polypropylene = 8 tonnes/7.9 tons; polyethylene = 6 tonnes/5.9 tons; and Dyneema/Admiral 2000/Spectra = a stupendous 20 tonnes/19.7 tons. Even the best manila would have to be nearly twice that size (and four times as strong) to match those figures.

♦ LEFT
Vegetable fibre cordage is much weaker and generally has a shorter life than synthetic products.

Synthetic cordage is much stronger and generally has a longer life than products made from vegetable fibre.

Comparing and Contrasting Natural Fibre and Synthetic Fibre Ropes

	NATURAL FIBRES				SYNTHETIC FIBRES			
	Sisal	Cotton	Hemp	Manilla	Polyethylene	Polypropylene	Polyester	Polyamide
Shock loading	●	●	●●●	●●	●	●●●	●●	●●●●
Handling	●	●●●●	●●●	●●	●●●	●●●	●●●●	●●●●
Durability	●	●●	●●●●	●●●	●●	●●●	●●●●	●●●●
Rot & mildew resistance	●	●	●	●	●●●●	●●●●	●●●●	●●●●
U.V. resistance	●●●●	●●●●	●●●●	●●●●	●●	●	●●●●	●●
Acid resistance	●	●	●	●	●●●●	●●●●	●●●●	●●●
Alkali resistance	●●	●●	●●	●●	●●●●	●●●●	●●●●	●●●●
Abrasion resistance	●●	●●	●●●	●●●	●●	●●	●●●●	●●●●
Storage	dry	dry	dry	dry	wet or dry	wet or dry	wet or dry	wet or dry
Buoyancy	sinks	sinks	sinks	sinks	floats (just)	floats	sinks	sinks
Melting point*	not affected	not affected	not affected	not affected	about 128°C (about 262°F)	about 150°C (about 302°F)	about 245°C (about 473°F)	about 250°C (about 482°F)

Key: ● poor ●● acceptable ●●● good ●●●● excellent
* Note that cordage softens and weakens at perhaps 20–30 per cent lower temperatures.

SUMMARY

These data take no account of fair wear and tear (including knots), damage or misuse (e.g. shock loading, or excessive friction). Consequently a safe working load will be considerably less – perhaps a fifth to a seventh of the quoted strengths. Then again, it is often necessary to buy synthetic cordage many times stronger than actually required; for example, a 4 mm/⅙ in cord would not match a block and tackle made for 25 mm/1 in rope even though it might be able to cope with the intended load, nor could it be comfortably grasped in the hand and heaved.

Knot tyers do not normally need to know either the molecular structure of cordage or its test data interpreted in charts and graphs. Cavers and climbers, flyers (of gliders and microlight aircraft), and all who calculatingly engage in potentially hazardous pursuits – from astronautics to undersea exploration – can obtain these technical details from the manufacturers. For the average user, a general knowledge of the main types of cordage is all that is needed to buy shrewdly and sensibly.

Care of Cordage

Do not leave rope or smaller stuff (cotton, thread or string) exposed needlessly to bright sunlight. Avoid any chemical contamination (for example, car battery acid). Protect synthetics from heat-generating friction, spark-spitting camp-fires or acetylene-cutting torches, and all other kinds of combustion. Try to avoid letting wet rope freeze. Store cordage in a dark, dry and cool place with good air circulation; relative humidity should be 40–60 per cent and the temperature 10–20°C (50–70°F). Wash dirty ropes in warm water to remove abrasive grit from their fibres and then dry them gently; similarly, at the end of a sailing season, soak and rinse in fresh water ropes that have been exposed to salt crystals. Abrasion can result from careless

◆ ABOVE
WRAPPED & REEF KNOTTED COIL
Rope and smaller cordage alike may be transported this way, in a bag or the boot (trunk) of a motor vehicle, with a realistic hope that it may be retrieved tangle-free at the end of the journey.

◆ LEFT
ALPINE COIL
Climbers favour this means of carrying their ropes.

handling in a rough environment or from ill-fitting blocks, cleats, or fairleads, but fair wear and tear is inevitable, whether it is from regular use or from being kept in the same position for prolonged periods. Even unused rope that has been carefully stored will age and become less reliable.

INSPECTING ROPES
Inspect ropes periodically, metre by metre/yard by yard in a good light, for loose, worn and broken surface yarns and cut strands. Some surface fluffing is inevitable; it is fairly harmless and might actually afford slight protection from further wear. Chemical attack can show as staining and

✦ BELOW
FIGURE-OF-EIGHT COIL
Storekeepers prefer this method, which provides a loop for hanging ropes.

✦ BELOW
FIREMAN'S COIL
Elegantly simple, this method deserves to be better known.

used with lifting tackle must be pensioned off long before they reach such senescence. Each rope should have its own log book in which its working history is recorded. Communal club ropes (that anyone might use at any time) should be retired after two or three years, but individually owned and maintained ropes may be used for four to five years, then down-graded for teaching knots and other points of general use that do not involve climbing.

It has been observed that rope with a mind of its own, awkward to manipulate and a trifle disobedient, is generally at the height of its powers. By contrast, rope that is soft and amenable, a pleasure to handle, should be condemned and discarded. There is some truth in this. Do not tread on rope, allow it to be nipped or become kinked, or drop it from a height. Coil ropes loosely and then hang them up on pegs well above the floor.

softening. Heat damage is harder to identify, unless fusing and glazing are detectable. Internal wear and damage can be seen by carefully opening laid strands but may be concealed in braided stuff (when the core could be weakened while the sheath remains relatively unworn and lacks obvious damage).

So a risk assessment for braided lines must also take into account their recent history of use and abuse. Worn-out rope looks its age. It is often attenuated (weakened by stretching), with a reduced diameter and a more acute angle of lay between the strands. Sheath-and-core ropes can develop creep, the sheath moving separately from the heart strands. Climbing ropes and those

Tools

◆ BELOW
Tying elaborate knots is made easier
with one or more handy tools (see key
to illustration).

Acquire a sharp and robust craft knife to cut rope and cord; scissors work only on thin strings and twines. Most of the knots in this book can be tied and tightened with just the fingers, aided now and then with a prod from the pointed cap of a ballpoint pen. A few (such as the Turk's heads) are more easily completed with one or more of the following tools.

GRIPFIDS

Handmade by rope craftsman Stuart Grainger, these resemble small Swedish fids, with the refinement that the tip clings to working strands, pulling them through knotwork as the tool is withdrawn. Two sizes cope with cordage up to either 7 mm/³⁄₁₀ in or 12 mm/½ in diameter.

NETTING NEEDLES

These serve as bobbins for storing quantities of small cords tangle-free and ready for immediate use. Sizes range from a tiny 11.5 cm/4½ in to jumbo-sized ones 30 cm/12 in or more in length. Shun crudely made ones in favour of those that are polished to a smooth finish. The seller will show you how to load them.

ROUND-BILLED PLIERS

Handy for tightening knots with lots of crossing points. Most high street hardware shops or do-it-yourself superstores will have them. Choose a pair to suit the scale of work: a small size (sometimes called "jeweller's

pliers") will have an overall length of about 10 cm/4 in, with more robust sizes from about 15 cm/6 in upwards.

SWEDISH FIDS*

These are used to poke and prize open gaps through which working strands can be tucked and pulled. Obtainable from yacht chandlers and serious rope stockists, they range in length from about 15 cm/6 in to 38 cm/15 in or more. Choose a size to match the scale of your work.

WIRE LOOPS

Homemade from stiff and springy wire 0.25 cm/¹⁄₁₀ in diameter – or thinner – inserted securely into a handle, these are indispensable alternatives to fids when working with smaller stuff.

KEY TO TOOLS	
1	Netting needle (large)
2	Netting needle (medium)
3	Netting needle (small)
4	Gripfid (large)
5	Gripfid (small)
6	Hollow "Swedish" fid (small)
7	Hollow "Swedish" fid (large)
8	Homemade wire loop (large)
9	Homemade wire loop (small)
10	Homemade wire loop (medium)
11	Jeweller's pliers
12	Round-billed pliers

* Originally fids were solid hardwood spikes. They can occasionally be found in antique shops or markets as collectable treen (lathe-turned wood).

Cutting & Securing Ends

TYING & TAPING

Before cutting any natural fibre cordage, first tape or tie it to prevent fraying. Adhesive tape is the least attractive option – and unacceptable on finished craftwork – but it is used a lot in preparatory stages as an easy alternative to whipping. Wrap where the cut is to be made and then simply slice the tape in half to achieve two bound ends at a stroke. Alternatively, tie a pair of strangle or constrictor knots, one on either side of where the cut is to be made.

HEATING & SEALING

This is now widely practised by ropeworkers and riggers. There is no need to tape or tie heat-sealed ends. Rope manufacturers and stockists have electrically heated guillotines to cut-and-seal the ropes and cords they sell. These cost too much for most of us, so the comparatively cool yellow flame of a struck match may have to do on small stuff. For large diameters, or to cut-and-seal a batch of strands, heat the blade of an old penknife in the blue flame of a blow-torch until the tip and edge glow cherry-red. Pause to re-heat it every few seconds for a clean and fast cut. Nylon melts, drips and burns with whitish smoke and a smell said to resemble fish or celery; it may even flash into a small flame (easily blown out). Polyester melts, drips and burns with dense black smoke and a smell like mushrooms. Polypropylene and

TYING

1 Tie two constrictor knots, one either side of where the cut will be made.

2 Slice vertically down halfway between the two binding knots already tied.

TAPING

1 Wrap a turn or two of adhesive tape around the rope or cord.

2 Cut vertically down through the middle of the taped portion.

HEAT SEALING 1

With an electric guillotine or a heated knife blade (not shown), cordage and small diameter ropes may be neatly cut and sealed.

HEAT SEALING 2

Use the naked flame of a match or cigarette lighter for a quick but often lumpy seal.

polyethylene react at lower temperatures, shrinking rapidly away from the source of heat. It is possible to pinch the soft heated ends to a point, rolling them between forefinger and thumb, before they harden, but take care

to wet the fingertips first or it may cause a burn and blister. A cord that appears to be synthetic but actually chars and even ignites without melting, is probably made from rayon, which comes from wood pulp.

Terms & Techniques

Anyone who ties a knot is described in knotting circles as a tyer (not tier) since the former is unambiguous while the latter has a different meaning when written.

SIMPLE TERMS

The end actively involved in the tying process is referred to as the **working end** or sometimes – by anglers – as the **tag end**; the in-active remainder is known as the **standing part** and **standing end**. Doubling a line so that two parts are brought close together creates a **bight**. If this is done to locate the exact centre of the bit of stuff in hand, then one is said to **middle** it. Once the two adjacent parts cross, a bight turns into a loop; a further twist creates a couple of **elbows**, while the process of turning a bight or loop into an improvised eye by wrapping the end several times around the standing part is referred to as **dogging**. Any loop that is pulled

so small that it deforms and damages a rope becomes a **kink**.

The word **rope** is generally defined as meaning any plaited, braided or laid (in strands) product over 10 mm ($5/12$ in) in diameter, although there are exceptions (for example, some climbing ropes are 9 mm/$3/8$ in diameter). Anything much smaller is referred to as **cord**, **string**, **twine** or **thread**. Rope and cord are collectively called **cordage** but, more commonly, **stuff**. A rope or cord dedicated to a particular job becomes a **line** (tow line, washing line, lifeline, throwing or heaving line), or acquires an even more specific label (lanyard, lashing or lassoo). A lightweight throwing or heaving line that is used to haul a heavier line across an intervening space is known as a **messenger**. The terms **plait** and **braid** are virtually interchangeable. There are, however, some who say that braids are flat while plaits have a three-dimensional cross-section.

Ropeworkers often "take a **turn**" in order to check a load by means of the friction it applies. Wrapping the working end an extra amount to bring it alongside the standing part, so as to tie it off, produces a **round turn**. Converting a single-ply knot to two, three (or more) ply involves following the original **lead** of the knot around with the working end. The place within a knot where the collective friction of its parts is concentrated is known as the **nip**. The tuck that finally secures a knot, preventing it from collapsing or unravelling, is the **locking tuck**. A simple loop is an **overhand loop** when the working end lies on top of the standing part, becoming an **underhand loop** if the working end goes beneath the standing part.

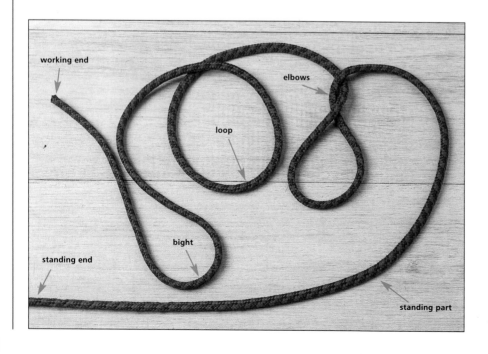

working end

elbows

loop

bight

standing end

standing part

1 More often than not, a clove hitch may have been tied with the working end.

2 But slide the knot sideways off its foundation – and it will fall apart.

3 Once separated from its foundation, nothing remains of the knot but the line in which it was tied.

4 To re-tie the clove hitch, this time in the bight, first cast an overhand loop.

5 Create a second underhand loop immediately alongside the first one.

6 Twist the loops to overlap them. The resulting clove hitch may be slid back on to its foundation.

TYING TECHNIQUES

Most knots can be tied in more than one way. The methods illustrated have been chosen either because they are easier to learn or to photograph clearly. Practised knot tyers develop more dextrous ways to tie knots that are almost sleight of hand. Discover these slicker and quicker tying tricks for yourself: with a completed knot in your hands, back-track, untying the knot a step at a time, to see how it is created. A short cut may occur to you. Re-tie it that way in future.

Tying a knot "in the bight" means doing so without using the working end. When a hitch or a binding knot collapses to nothing if slid from the foundation around which it was tied or a loop knot can be unravelled without recourse to its ends (in other words, it "unties in the bight"), then it can be tied in the bight. This is the "law of hitch & bight" proposed by Harry Asher in the mid-1980s. A surprising number of knots may be tied this way. Knowing the principle can also enable knot tyers to spot subtle differences in seemingly identical knots: for example, the bag knot can be tied in the bight but the miller's knot cannot.

Most knots must be drawn up gradually so as to remove slack and daylight before gently pulling on each end and standing part in turn to create a knot that remains snug and firm.

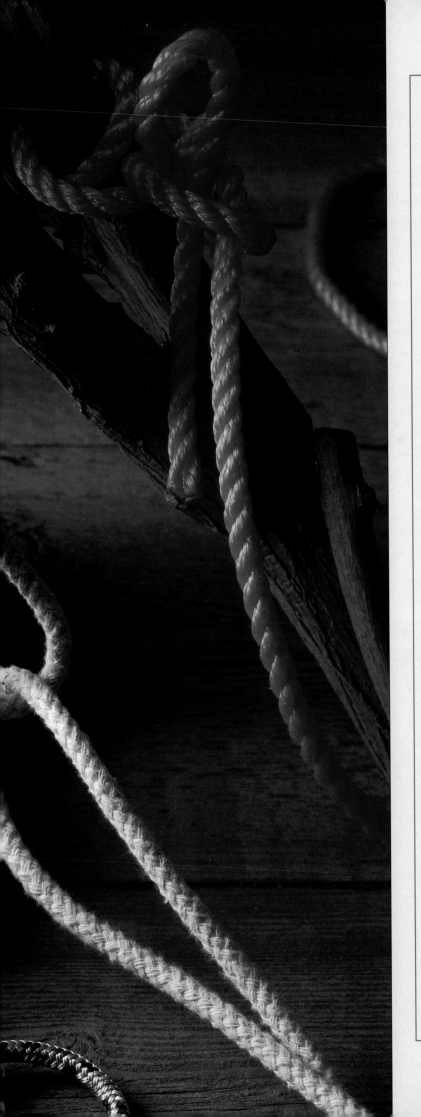

BASIC KNOTS, BENDS & HITCHES

"Every knot is an exercise in friction ... extreme simplicity can only be had at the expense of effectiveness."

(BRION TOSS –
THE RIGGER'S APPRENTICE, 1984)

All knotting may be summed up under three main headings: Knots, Bends and Hitches. A hitch attaches a line to a post, rail, spar, ring or even another rope; a bend joins two ropes together; a knot is anything other than a bend or a hitch (including stopper knots, binding knots and loop knots) although the word "knot" is also used, sometimes confusingly, in a general way to refer even to bends and hitches. Discover how easily you can tie these 20 basic knots. All you will need is two lengths of flexible cord, each 1–2 m/3–6½ ft long and from 5–10 mm/ ⅕–⁵⁄₁₂ in in diameter.

Most cordage will fray unless the ends are securely treated in some way. A better-looking treatment than taping, tying and heat sealing is a whipping of some kind, and four whipped ends are detailed in this section.

Simple, Overhand or Thumb Knot

This is the most elementary stopper knot, to prevent small stuff (cotton, thread or string) from fraying or pulling out of a hole through which it has been threaded. Its uses range from securing thread in a needle to tying loose change into the corner of a handkerchief when on the beach or anywhere else where deep pockets are temporarily not available. Nobody ever has to be taught to tie this knot. It just comes naturally.

1 Make an overhand loop in the small stuff that is to be tied.

2 Tuck the working end through the loop already formed and pull on the standing end to tighten the knot.

Overhand Knot with Drawloop

Drawloops act as quick releases, and may also strengthen some knots by bulking them up with an extra knot part. Overlooked and underrated by many knot tyers, drawloops deserve to be used more, and will from time to time be recommended in this book.

Start to tie a simple overhand knot but stop before the working end has been fully pulled through.

Two Strand Overhand Knot

This is another knot that the youngest person can tie instinctively. It creates a bigger stopper knot, for cottons or domestic string, and also acts to hold cords together as long as they lie in the same direction, for example, to prevent a waist tie in pyjamas, swimming trunks or tracksuit trousers (sweatpants) from pulling out when not in use. NB: This is not a bend because the two cords are not aligned to be pulled in opposite directions.

1 Place the two strings or cords to be tied parallel and together.

2 Tie a simple overhand knot. Tighten, taking care to keep the lines parallel (like railway tracks) throughout.

Double Overhand Knot

This forms a chunkier stopper knot than the simple overhand knot, although it will not block a larger hole. It is, however, an indispensable technique for other knots that are based upon it.

1 Tie an overhand knot – but tuck the working end a second time.

2 Gently pull both ends apart, at the same time twisting them in opposite directions. In the example shown, the lefthand thumb goes up and away from the tyer, the righthand thumb down and away. The cord dictates what it wants to do; simply go along with it. See how a diagonal knot part wraps itself around – let it happen. Pull on both ends at the same time to tighten this knot.

Triple (and Multiple) Overhand Knots

Three (or more) initial tucks produce triple or multiple overhand knots. These can make shortenings and embellishments, such as those seen in the ropes around the waists of nuns and monks, who used this triple knot as a symbolic reference to their threefold sacred vows.

2 Pull both ends, rotating them in different directions so that a diagonal wrapping turn appears.

1 Tie a double overhand knot, then tuck the working end a third time.

3 Shape the emerging knot to bed all of the knot parts down snugly. Tighten by pulling both ends apart.

Strangle Knot

A double overhand knot, tied around something, makes a strangle knot. Use it to seize cut ends of cordage and prevent them from fraying; to secure rolls of anything from carpets to technical drawings and wallpaper, or to clamp do-it-yourself and hobbyists' bits-and-pieces together while the glue hardens. Several other useful binding knots are featured in this book; but, for a start, this one is as good as any. Try it also with a drawloop.

1 Produce a double overhand knot but at this stage keep it very loose.

2 Insert whatever is to be bound, ensure the overriding diagonal lies between the other two knot parts, and tighten the knot by pulling on both ends. The ends can then be cut off short.

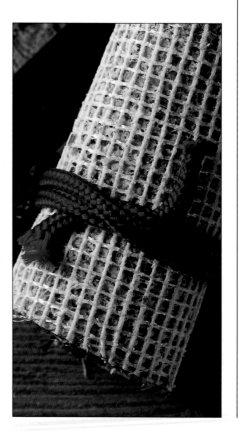

Single Hitch

Commonly referred to as a half hitch, alone this is an unreliable means of attachment except for the most temporary and trivial of purposes (when a drawloop might help) but it is the means of finishing off other more substantial working hitches.

1 Tie the ubiquitous overhand knot around something firm, such as a fat felt tip pen, to discover how this careful rearrangement traps the working end.

2 Leave a longer working end, which is not completely pulled through, for a drawloop.

Two Half Hitches

Two half hitches are the tried and trusted way to secure a line to a ring, rail or anything. They are always identical, i.e. the working end goes the same way around the standing part in both cases.

1 Tie a single half hitch with the working end of the line.

2 Add an identical second half hitch and draw them snugly together to complete this useful attachment.

Round Turn & Two Half Hitches

This is a classic hitch, comparatively strong and secure, the name of which describes it exactly. It can be used to secure a boat, to tow a broken-down vehicle or secure a load.

1 Take a turn around the anchorage, bring the working end alongside the standing part, and apply a half hitch.

2 Add an identical half hitch to complete this dependable knot.

Overhand Knot & Half Hitch

This loop knot has been used by weavers to rig looms, by Inuits (Eskimos) to string bows, by anglers as a leader loop for tackle, and for starting to tie parcels. It is sometimes called a packer's knot.

1 Tie an overhand knot with a large drawloop and adjust the loop to the required size.

2 Wrap and tuck a half hitch with the working end around the standing part. Tighten by pulling on each one of the loop legs in turn.

Overhand Loop

Use this very basic knot in thin stuff for starting parcels and other lashings. It does not easily untie and is therefore a knot that must generally be cut off and discarded after use.

1 Double one end of a cord (make a bight) and form a loop in the doubled end.

2 Tie an overhand knot, taking the trouble to keep the knot parts neatly parallel throughout the knot. Tighten by pulling on each one of the four knot parts in turn.

Double Overhand Loop

This loop is bulkier and slightly stronger than the previous one.

Do not attempt to untie it – cut it off after use.

1 With a somewhat longer bight, tie a double overhand knot.

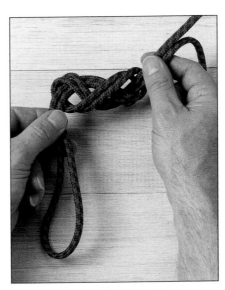

2 Uncross any twisted knot parts and remove any slack until the knot assumes its characteristic shape. Then tighten gradually, pulling on each of the four knot parts in turn.

Surgeon's Loop

This is a triple overhand loop, stronger for the extra tuck, and is recommended for angling lines.

Make this knot in dispensable stuff as it is easier to cut it off than to untie it.

1 Make a fairly long bight and tie a treble overhand knot in it.

2 Eliminate any unevenness and mould it with your fingers into a smooth barrel-shaped knot. Anglers may spit on monofilaments to lubricate them.

Simple Noose

This simplest of running (sliding) loops is useful to start parcels or other lashings.

Working away from the short end, tie an overhand knot (with drawloop) in what would normally be regarded as the standing part of the line, and pull it tight.

Scaffold Knot

This is a strong, secure sliding loop. Use it when an eye must be protected from chafe by means of a metal or plastic liner (called a "thimble"). Tighten the loop to grip and hold this particular bit of hardware. With practised fingers, this knot can be tied in no more than 30 seconds and the beauty of it is that the more the strain that's put on it, the tighter this knot will grip.

1 Make a bight and tie a double overhand knot with the working end around the standing part of the line.

2 Pull the end and the appropriate leg of the loop in opposite directions to tighten the knot.

Multiple Scaffold Knot

A triple overhand knot will make a double scaffold knot, which is perhaps slightly stronger. A multiple knot results from a multiple overhand knot, but there is probably little benefit from doing this other than to produce a handsomely handy bulk.

1 Tie a straight forward triple overhand knot in the working end around the standing part.

2 Pull the end and the appropriate loop leg in opposite directions to tighten the knot.

Overhand Bend

Also known as the tape knot, this knot is recommended for the flat or tubular woven webbing (tape) used by cavers and climbers – although it works in anything from the largest cables to the finest angling monofilaments.

2 Follow the lead of the original knot with the second working end.

1 Tie an overhand knot in the end of one of the two lines to be joined. Insert the end of the second line.

3 For a twofold knot, ensure that all knot parts are parallel and that the short ends emerge at the top of the knot as there is some evidence that it may be stronger this way. Pull the standing parts to tighten.

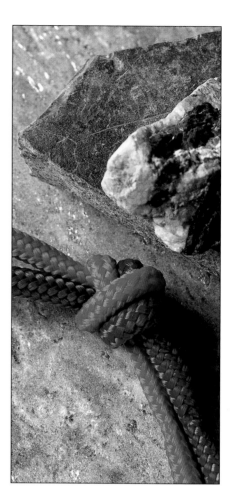

Fisherman's Knot

The reliable fisherman's knot can be used for anything and everything from domestic to heavy industrial tasks. This is a knot that can be untied if it has been made from rope, but if you make it out of string you will have to cut it off.

1 Lay the two lines parallel and close to one another, tying an overhand knot with one end around the standing part of the other.

2 Turn the half-completed knot end-for-end and tie an identical overhand knot with the other end. Pull first on both working ends to tighten the individual knots, then on the standing parts to unite and tighten the knot.

Double Fisherman's Knot

The stronger double fisherman's knot is known to anglers as a grinner knot (presumably because of the gaping mouth formed before the knots slide shut). It is a reasonably secure knot.

1 Place the two lines parallel and close together, tying a double overhand knot with one working end around the other standing part.

2 Turn the half-completed knot end-for-end and tie a second double overhand knot with the other end. Tighten individual knots before pulling on the standing parts to close the knot.

Triple Fisherman's Knot

A triple fisherman's knot is an angler's double grinner knot and is used for thinner, springier or more slippery lines.

Proceed as for a double fisherman's knot – but use triple overhand knots – and tighten similarly.

Strength & Security

Knots weaken the rope, cord or string in which they are tied. An unwanted overhand knot allowed to remain in a fishing line or washing line, for instance, will more than halve the breaking strength. Bulky knots are better, the double fisherman's or grinner knot preserving 65 to 70 per cent of the cordage strength and the blood knot 85 to 90 per cent; while the bimini twist is claimed by some to be 100 per cent efficient (in other words, as strong as the unknotted line). Climbers, whose lives literally hang upon their knots; anglers, keen to preserve expensive tackle and to catch that record-breaking fish; ropeworking assault, rescue or survey teams; lifting tackle operatives on construction sites – all choose and use strong knots.

Security is a different consideration. A strong knot that slips and slides, spills, capsizes or otherwise comes undone, is less secure than one that holds firm. Some knots are secure enough when carefully assembled and placed under a steady load but loosen and come adrift if intermittently jerked or repeatedly shaken.

Since strength and security are different characteristics, knots that combine both of them would seem to be ideal – why bother with any others? This is because ease of tying and untying are often essential. Simplicity too may be desirable. So, when they can get away with it, knot tyers knowingly trade off one quality

against the other. Indeed some classic knots, despite long established reputations for reliability, are surprisingly weak and insecure when put to the test. The common bowline is barely 45 per cent strong and in stiff or slick rope can easily be made to spill.

✦ ABOVE
Strengthened bowline secured with an overhand knot.

Knots can be made more secure. For example, the relatively strong figure-of-eight loop may be made more secure by attaching the short end of the rope to its adjacent standing part with a double overhand knot (*above left*). Similarly, the common bowline may be both strengthened and made more secure with the extra turn of this double (or climber's) version, the working end of which is further safeguarded with an overhand knot to the nearest leg of the loop (*left*). The reef knot is essentially weak, but the two ends may be secured with a couple of double overhand knots (*above centre*). A proprietary brand of chock (*above right*), known as a "wallnut" and used for mountaineering and related activities, is attached to a strop made from outstandingly strong Spectra accessory cord. This is tied with a double fisherman's knot. Security is assured by taping both ends to their adjacent standing parts.

Common Whipping

Comparatively quick to apply, this traditional treatment for a rope's end is also the most likely to come untied.

WHIPPINGS

Whipping twines are sold by rope stockists. Use natural (vegetable) fibre for natural fibre ropes and synthetic on synthetic ropes. Whipped ends should not be heat-sealed. The illustration samples have been made with thicker cords, for clarity, than would really be used.

1 Make a long bight and lay it along the rope as shown.

2 Begin to wrap the working end around the rope, trapping both legs of the bight within the initial turn. Wrapping turns are made in the opposite direction to the lay of the rope, so that any tendency for the rope to unlay will tighten the whipping.

3 Continue to wrap tightly towards the rope's end, taking care to keep each turn snugly and neatly against the preceding one. Continue until the whipping is at least as long as the diameter of the rope.

4 *(left)* Tuck the working end through the remaining portion of the bight.

5 *(right)* Pull the working end (not illustrated) to reduce the bight until it traps the working end; then pull harder, so that the working end is dragged beneath the wrapping turns. Stop when the interlocked elbows reach the centre of the whipping. If they saw through and break the twine, either wrap less tightly or use stronger stuff; in any case they make a bulge beneath the wrapping turns. Trim the ends.

Perfected Whipping

This improved version eliminates the harsh elbows that are a feature of the common whipping.

1 Lay both ends of the whipping twine together, pointing in opposite directions, on the rope.

2 Begin to wrap with that part of the twine furthest from the rope's end.

3 Continue to wrap as tightly and neatly as possible, keeping the two underlying twine parts parallel and together, and untangling the working bight (each completed revolution) from the rope's end.

4 As the working bight shrinks, remove the twist that is inevitably imparted to it (better still, with practice, at the start insert a counter-twist that will unwind as the work progresses).

5 Pull on the end of the twine to remove all slack from the final wrapping turn, before pulling steadily on both ends to secure and finish off the whipping.

West Country Whipping

Some dismiss this as ugly and not a proper whipping. It is certainly not as neat as other whippings, but more pragmatic knot tyers point out that it stays put when a common whipping comes undone. In practice, the alternate half knots, with repetition, begin to take on a rugged bumpiness that is not unattractive.

1 Tie an overhand knot about 2.5 cm/ 1 in from the rope's end.

2 Turn the rope face down and tie an identical second overhand knot on the reverse side.

3 Turn the work face up again, and tie a third overhand knot alongside the first one. Repeat this process of simple knotting on alternate sides.

4 Finish off with a reef (square) knot, and poke the ends back beneath the completed whipping with a handy pointed implement.

Sailmaker's Whipping

No matter how well tied, after much wear and tear, whippings do inevitably come loose and come off. For ropes that flog about in the wind, such as flag halyards and running rigging aboard sailing craft, this tough variant is tied into the rope's strands, which gives it extra strength and security. Alternatively, on braided rope, the riding turns that secure it may be stitched right through with a robust needle.

1 Unlay the rope's end for a distance of about 5 cm/2 in and pass a bight of whipping twine over one strand, so that both ends of the twine emerge between the other two strands.

2 Re-lay the strands and select either end of the twine with which to begin the whipping.

3 Wrap neatly and tightly from the bight towards the rope's end.

4 Continue until the length of the whipping at least equals the diameter of the rope.

5 Lay the bight along the rope so that it spirals with one leg following each of the grooves created by the strand it originally enclosed.

6 Loop the bight over the strand and pull it tight with the standing end of the twine.

7 Lay this end of the twine in a similar helix along the remaining third groove.

8 Tie the two ends securely between the strands, preferably with a reef (square) knot. (Note – A granny knot was used here, as it was easier to conceal in the picture of the finished whipping, given the thick cord.)

BENDS

*"To bend two Cabells or Roapes together . . .
when we meane to take them a-sunder againe."*

(Sir Henry Manwayring –
The Sea-man's Dictionary, 1644)

A bend is any knot that joins two ropes or
other lines together. As a general rule, it should
be possible to untie bends after use, for rope is
a costly item that may be re-used later for
another purpose. Restrict untieable knots to
string, anglers' monofilaments and other such
stuff, from which they can be cut off and
discarded when no longer needed. Most bends
are made in two separate ends of identical
material but some, for example a sheet bend
and the different heaving line bends, are
intended for use when two lines differ
noticeably in diameter or stiffness. The
lightweight binding knots that join the two
ends of the same length of line (for example.
parcel twine or shoe laces) are knots – as
opposed to bends – but in more substantial
stuff bends are employed to create cargo
strops and endless slings for caving
and climbing.

Flemish Bend

Old seamen viewed this bend with disfavour, because it tended to jam in natural fibre ropes, but it suits synthetic cordage. Climbers like it because it is easily learned and readily checked by a team leader.

1 Make a loop in one end of one of the two lines to be joined.

2 Impart half a twist, in this instance left thumb going up and away – that is, anticlockwise (counterclockwise).

3 Tuck the working end as shown to create the characteristic figure-of-eight outline.

4 Introduce the second line, with its working end parallel to and alongside the first one.

5 Follow the lead of the first rope with the second, keeping to the outside of the first bend (evidence suggests that this makes a stronger knot).

6 Continue around and through the original knot, transferring to the inside of the second bend.

7 Complete the two-ply knot, then tighten it a bit at a time by pulling on each working end and standing part in turn.

Double Figure-of-Eight Bend

This knot is similar in function to the fisherman's knot but, unlike that knot, it is bilaterally symmetrical (both sides look the same). Several knots with a figure-of-eight layout are referred to as Flemish knots, and an alternative name for this one is the Flemish bend. Leave the knots a few inches apart for a knot that will absorb a sudden jerk or snatch by sliding before it holds.

1 Tie a figure-of-eight knot in one of the two lines and insert the second line through the first knot.

2 Then begin to tie another figure-of-eight knot.

3 Complete the second figure-of-eight knot, which, when the work is turned end-for-end, must be identical to the first one.

4 Pull first on the working ends to remove the slack from the individual knots, then on both standing parts to slide them together.

Linfit Knot

Thick and springy materials need an alternative to the double fisherman's (or grinner) knot, and this one was devised by angler Owen K. Nuttall.

1 Make a bight in each of the two lines to be joined and lay them one across the other, as shown.

2 Take the working end of the upper line around the back of the lower bight from right to left.

3 Bring the working end of the lower line across the front, taking it from left to right.

4 Pass the lefthand working end in a clockwise direction around the lefthand standing part.

5 Tuck this lefthand working end from behind and bring it up through the lefthand bight.

6 Bring the righthand working end anticlockwise (counterclockwise) around the righthand standing part.

7 Tuck this working end from in front down through the righthand bight. Remove the slack from this arrangement until you have a symmetrical form, with both ends emerging at right angles to the standing parts and on the same side of the knot. Pull on each working and standing end in turn to tighten the completed knot.

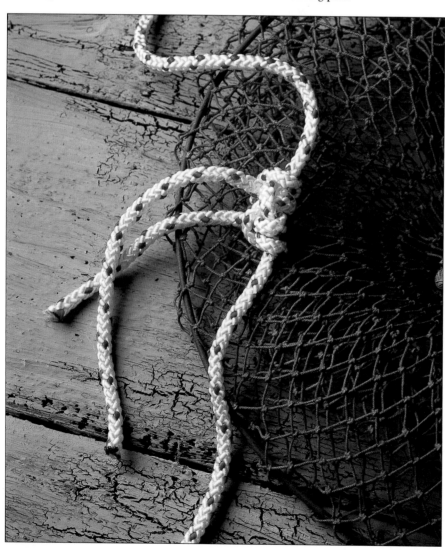

Strop Bend

Any two eyes, loops and endless strops or slings may be interlaced this way. It can amuse young children to make long multi-coloured chains of elastic bands with a series of these knots; but the strop bend can also be put to hard labour on construction sites and dockyards.

1 Bring together two bights and insert one up through the other.

2 Double the working bight of the two back upon itself.

3 Pick up the standing parts of the working loop to draw them through the secondary loop.

4 Pull the remainder of the working loop completely through itself.

5 Begin to pull the two bights in opposite directions, one away from the other.

6 Continue until the two bights are snugly interlocked with one another.

7 Tighten by pulling on both pairs of loop legs at once. While this knot resembles a reef (square) knot in layout, the dynamics are very different, and it will, of course, only come undone if one of the lines breaks.

Blood Knot with Inward Coil

This is one of the several classic angling knots that, because of their numerous compact wrapping turns, are collectively known as blood or barrel-shaped knots. Numerous wrapping turns make this knot both strong and secure. It is primarily used by anglers, who tie it in their fine lines, but it can prove equally useful, tied in thicker cordage, out of water.

1 Bring two lines, facing in opposite directions, close together, and lay them parallel.

2 With one of the working ends, begin to apply wrapping turns.

3 The first wrap should go around the front and then down the back of both lines.

4 Ensure that the first wrapping turn encloses both of the lines to be joined so as to trap its own standing part.

5 Try to make each wrapping turn lie snugly and tightly beside the previous one.

6 Complete five or six turns, then tuck and trap the working end between both lines.

7 With the other working end, begin the wrapping process again.

8 Repeat the previous steps, wrapping in towards the middle of the emerging knot.

9 Finally tuck the second working end down through the centre of the knot (in the opposite direction to the other end). Mould all of the turns tight, from the outside in, and then pull on the two ends to remove any slack.

Carrick Bend with Ends Opposed

This knot name dates from the 18th century, but its actual origin is obscure. At Carrick-on-Suir in Ireland, the Elizabethan plasterwork of Ormonde Castle is embellished with numerous carrick bends moulded in relief, while a "carrack" was a type of medieval trading ship, from which perhaps comes Carrick Road outside Falmouth Harbour in Cornwall. Recommended for large hawsers and cables, this bend has acquired a reputation for strength, when it actually reduces the breaking strength of the ropes to about 65 per cent. Nevertheless, given today's strong synthetic cordages, it is still a considerable heavyweight among bends. It is said to be more secure if it is tied in such a way that the working ends emerge on opposite sides of the knot.

1 Make a loop with the working end of one of the two lines to be joined lying (in this instance) over its own standing part.

2 Place the second line over the initial loop, in the direction shown, and pass the working end beneath the other standing part.

3 Begin a second loop, taking the second working end over the first working end.

4 With the second end, make a locking tuck that goes under-over-under to complete the knot. Pull on the two standing parts to tighten the knot, when the flat heraldic outline will capsize into a compact and different form.

Carrick Bend with Ends Adjacent

With the ends on the same side of the knot, the carrick bend becomes the heraldic device once known as the Wake knot, the badge of the Saxon leader Hereward the Wake who in 1071 AD revolted against William the Conqueror. The late Desmond Mandeville, who researched the relationships of bends for more than 25 years, discovered there was one knot to which all were related and to which every family tree he drew returned – this one. Use this knot for decorative purposes, retaining the flat and open layout. It can look most attractive when used as a curtain tie-back, to secure a dressing gown cord, or even on an antique chaise longue.

1 Make a loop with the working end of one of the two lines to be joined going over the standing part.

2 Lay the working end of the second line beneath the initial loop, pointing in the direction shown.

3 Bring the second working end over the other working end.

4 Begin a second loop by taking the second new working end under the other standing part.

5 Make a locking tuck that goes over-under-over to secure the lefthand half of the knot.

6 Unlike the ends opposed version, keep this knot flat and open.

Vice Versa

Some intractable materials – such as wet and slimy leather thongs or bungee (elastic) shock cord – are difficult to keep in place and slither out of other bends. They can, however, be tamed with this relatively new knot from the fertile mind of Harry Asher, first published in 1989. The extra security can only be achieved with the additional tucks and turns that are features of this knot.

1 Lay the two lines to be joined parallel and together.

2 Take the righthand working end and bring it beneath the other standing part.

3 Pass the end over the other line and then tuck it beneath itself.

4 Take the other working end to the left, over the first of the two lines.

6 Cross the righthand end over the lefthand end and tuck it through the lefthand loop alongside its own standing part. Similarly, take hold of what has become the righthand end.

7 Finally, tuck the remaining working end through the righthand loop alongside its own standing part. Gently pull on all four of the emerging lines at once to securely tighten this knot.

Sheet Bend

This knot is neither strong nor secure. It reduces the strength of lines by 55 per cent, and can spill if subject to spasmodic jerking. This said, it is part of every knot tyer's basic repertoire. When it attaches a lanyard to a loop it may be referred to as a becket hitch, and, tied (by a different method) in yarns, it is called the weaver's knot.

1 Create a bight in the end of one of the ropes to be tied.

2 Take the second rope and tuck it up through the bight.

3 Pass the working end beneath the bight.

4 Tuck the working end beneath itself in such a way that both short ends are located on the same side of the completed knot (with many materials, it seems to be more secure this way).

Double Sheet Bend

If the two lines are of dissimilar size or stiffness, make the bight in the bigger or tougher one, and tie this double sheet bend to counteract any tendency for it to straighten and so spill the knot. There is no need for a third tuck. If this knot is insufficient, try the racking bend.

1 Make a bight in the larger of the two ropes to be joined.

2 Take the second of the lines and tuck it up through the bight.

3 Bring the end around and beneath the bight in the other rope.

4 Tuck the working end beneath itself so that both short ends are located on the same side of the knot (with many materials it is more secure this way).

5 Bring the working end around and beneath the bight and its own standing line once again, keeping it to the right of the original pass.

6 Finally, tuck the end through alongside the initial tuck to complete the double knot.

One-Way Sheet Bend

When a sheet bend is likely to be dragged over or through obstructions, the two short ends can be streamlined by means of this adaption. Use this simple but effective modification for ropes that may be towed in water, passed through a rocky crevice or even exposed to gale-force winds. The three short ends should, of course, point away from the direction in which the knot is being pulled so that they will not be pulled by the current or catch against any rocks.

1 Make a bight with the working end of one of the two ropes to be joined.

2 Take the end of the other rope and tuck it up through the bight.

3 Pass the working end around and beneath the bight in the other rope.

4 Tuck the end beneath itself so both short ends are on the same side.

5 Then bring the working end around and back on itself again to make a figure-of-eight.

6 Finally, tuck the end beneath itself (as shown) and lay it alongside the two parts of the other rope. Tighten carefully so that all the knot parts bed down snugly together.

Simple Simon Over

This knot (and two variations of it) were devised by Harry Asher and published in 1989. It is especially effective in slick synthetic lines and, once mastered, it can be tied easily. It has rarely appeared in print, but it merits being more widely known as it is a useful knot to have at one's fingertips when faced with tying slippery, synthetic lines.

1 Make a bight in one of the two lines to be joined and bring the working end of the other line over it.

2 Tuck the working end down through the bight and bring it out to the left (in this instance), then take it over both bight legs and, in a snaking "Z" track, back again beneath them.

3 Lay the end back over its preceding part (the "over" of the knot name).

4 From the outside of the bight, tuck the working end up and through and finally lay it alongside its own standing part. Tighten gradually, working the slack out of the completed knot.

Simple Simon Under

This is a variation of the simple Simon over knot by Harry Asher. Although on first appearance, it does not look unlike the simple Simon over, it is more secure and can cope with dissimilar cord sizes and textures. This is an extremely useful knot that deserves more recognition as it is useful for slippery synthetic cord and should be used on a wider scale than it is at present.

1 Make a bight in one of the two lines to be joined and bring the working end of the other line over it.

2 Tuck the working end down through the bight and divert it to the left (in this instance) prior to going back over both bight legs.

3 Bring the working end back beneath both bight legs and then tuck it beneath its preceding part (the "under" of the knot name).

4 From the outside of the bight, tuck the working end up through and finally lay it alongside its own standing part. Tighten gradually, working the slack out of the completed knot.

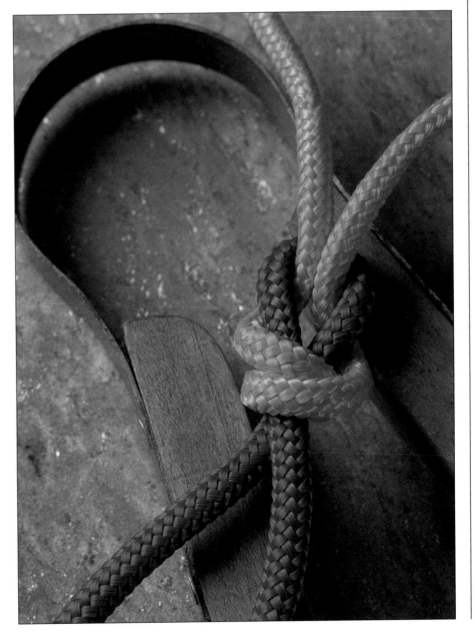

Simple Simon Double

This is a variation of the simple Simon knots of Harry Asher; it is even more secure and has the advantage that it can cope with a greater dissimilarity of cord sizes and textures.

1 Make a bight in the larger of the two lines to be joined and bring the working end of the other line over it.

2 Divert the working end (in this instance taking it to the left) beneath the bight.

3 Wrap the end over and then beneath both bight legs.

4 Take the working end back again so that it lies over both legs of the bight.

5 Pass the working end down beneath the bight over its own preceding standing part.

6 Carry the end across the front of the bight over its own standing part.

7 From the outside of the bight, finally tuck the working end through alongside its own standing part. Pull the knot snug and tight, taking care not to distort it in the process.

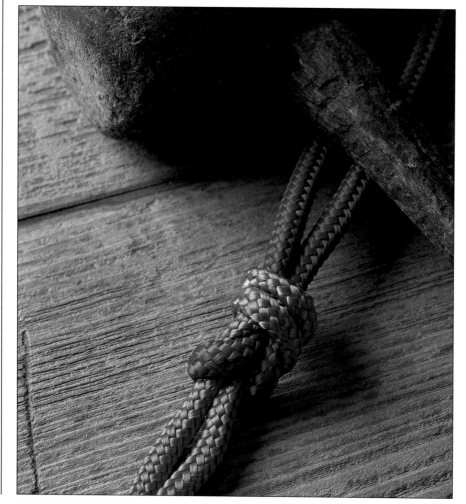

Shake Hands

This excellent knot is almost unknown, yet it is one of the best bends, being not only secure but also easily loosened and untied, and neat in appearance with the ends alongside the standing parts. Harry Asher devised it, influenced – admittedly – by Clifford Ashley's 1944 description of a similar layout as a loop knot.

1 Make a loop with one working end going over its own standing part.

2 Pass the other working end up through the initial loop and make a second loop (the end going under the standing part).

3 Take the first working end back down behind both of the loops in the developing knot.

4 Bring the first working end up through the common central space between both loops.

5 Now bring the first working end down in front of both loops.

6 Then tuck the second working end down through the common central space between both of the loops.

7 Pull on both working ends and standing parts in turn to tighten the knot.

Tumbling Thief Knot, Centre-tucked

This chunky knot, with both ends centrally nipped, is a good reason to learn the unreliable common thief knot described below.

1 Make a bight in one of the two lines to be joined. Bring the working end of the other line up through the bight and then divert it to the side of the bight where its short end is located.

2 Bring the working end down beneath both legs of the bight, and tuck the end back through the initial bight alongside its own standing part. This is the common thief knot.

3 Now begin to pull each of the working ends across to the opposite side of the knot.

4 Uncross the working cords to momentarily assume the loosely locked layout shown.

5 Cross the two working ends over precisely as shown. This is the tumbling thief, a relatively secure form of the thief knot if drawn tight.

6 Take the upper working end and tuck it directly down through the common central space of the existing knot.

7 Take the lower working end and tuck it up through the common central space. Pull on each one of the four cords in turn to tighten this knot.

Alpine Butterfly Bend

Cutting the loop off an Alpine butterfly knot produces this bend. Indeed, a lot of loop knots can be converted to useful bends this way, and knot tyers who have spotted and reported this principle include Brion Toss, Desmond Mandeville and Harry Asher. Tie it directly to bend together two lines.

1 Form an underhand loop with one of the two ends to be joined.

2 Form a similar underhand loop with the other end, interlocking it with the first loop, as shown.

3 Take either one of the two working ends and tuck it down through the central space common to both loops.

4 Then tuck the other working end down beside the first end, through the almost completed knot.

5 Pull gently on both working ends, then on the standing parts, to remove slack and tighten the knot.

Bowline Bend

In wet natural fibre ropes at sea, when even simple knots could be relied upon to hold, it was recommended that hawsers should be joined with a pair of interlocked bowlines, and that still holds good – literally – in some of today's cordage. The advantage of the bowline is that it does not slip or jam even under tension. This bend can be used for lines of dissimilar diameters, constructions and materials, but the two loops may be weakened where their interlinked elbows cross and rub against one another.

1 Make the initial overhand loop that will cinch the completed knot and tuck the working end up through it.

2 Pass the working end around behind the standing part of the line.

3 Tuck the working end down through the loop and pull the working end to tighten the knot.

4 Make an overhand loop with a second line and tuck the working end through the first bowline.

5 Pass the working end up through the second loop and under the standing part of the line.

6 Tuck this working end down through the second loop and pull the working end to tighten the knot.

Twin Bowline Bend

This alternative to the bowline bend avoids the sharp elbows of the latter knot and is stronger for that reason as it avoids the risk of chafing and rubbing.

1 Arrange the two lines parallel, with the working ends opposed.

2 Form the loop that is characteristic of bowlines in the standing part of one of the lines, as shown.

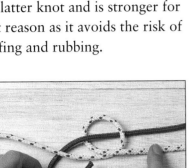

3 Tuck the other working end up through the loop and pass it around the back of the standing part.

4 Tuck the end down through the loop to complete the first bowline.

5 Turn the half-completed knot end-for-end and begin again with an identical loop.

6 Take the end and tuck it as before, up through the loop and around the standing part.

7 Tuck the end down through the loop to complete the second bowline, ensuring that the working ends are at least as long as those illustrated (and preferably longer). The standing parts will each take an equal part of the strain upon the loaded knot.

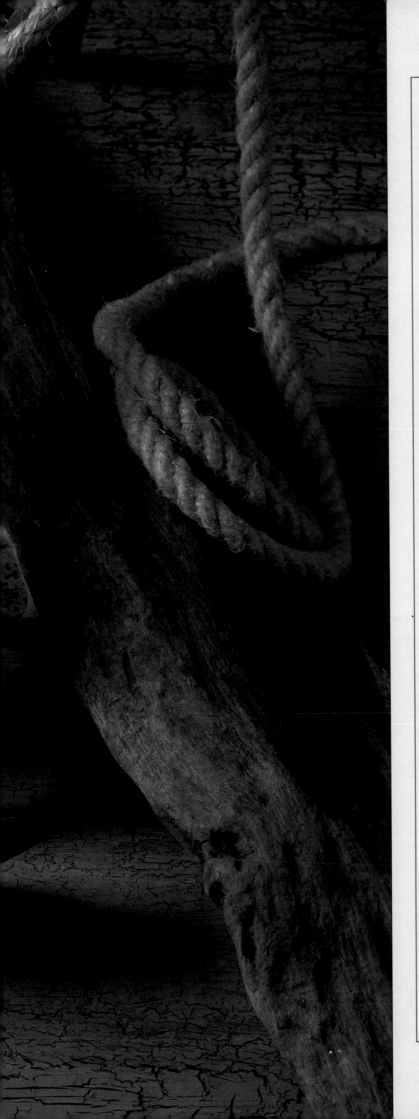

HITCHES

"Hitches are employed in making fast to such things as a pile, bitt, spar, rail, ring or hook, and . . . no one hitch will suffice for all."
(HERVEY GARRETT SMITH –
THE ARTS OF THE SAILOR, 1953)

A line is said to be "made fast" (not "hitched") to various objects, even another rope, and only the knot itself is called a hitch. Some hitches work best with a direct pull at right angles to the point of attachment; others will withstand a sideways or varying direction of pull; it is a rare and remarkable hitch indeed that can cope with a pull towards the point of a tapering foundation – but one is included in this section. The fisherman's or anchor bend and the gaff topsail halyard bend are actually hitches and so are included within this section. Their irregular names are due to old-time sailormen who, obeying a verbal quirk, always spoke of "bending" a line to a ring or spar. The ossel knot is also a hitch, but it is known as a knot since there is already an ossel hitch.

Pedigree Cow Hitch

This is a useful knot for a pull that is more or less at right angles to the point of attachment. Put it to work to start lashings or to suspend garden shed and garage impedimenta from the roof.

1 Take the working end around and down, from front to back of the anchorage point.

2 Bring the end around in front of its own standing part.

3 Take the end back up behind the foundation and bring it down in front once again.

4 Tuck the end through the bight, the result being a fairly useless common cow hitch.

5 Now tuck the working end back through the basic knot to secure and transform it.

Cow Hitch Variant

This is an even stronger and more secure version than the pedigree cow hitch. Although similar to the pedigree cow hitch, which was an innovation from the fresh mind of Harry Asher, the cow hitch variant was published in 1995 by Robert Pont of France, who first spotted it in Quebec and named it the Piwich knot after the child (Piwich Kust of the Bois Brule tribe) who tied it. Use it as a bag knot, or to suspend lockets, amulets and similar items of jewellery from a neck lanyard.

1 Take the working end once around the point of attachment.

2 Make a single half hitch with the working end around the line's standing part.

3 Take the working end across the front and pass it up (in this instance, to the left) behind the anchorage point.

4 Bring the working end down in front and tuck it down beside the standing part of the line, taking it through the enclosing turn.

Figure-of-Eight Hitch

A trivial holdfast for the odd undemanding job, this hitch is releatively simple and easy to master. The extra crossing point gives a bit more friction and hold than a single half hitch. It is more secure than a single half hitch, especially around an object with a small diameter, and could, of course, be used with a round turn, but always treat it with caution as it does not have the strength of many other hitches.

1 Pass the working end of the line around the anchorage point from front to back.

2 Bring the end forward and across the standing part (in this instance, from right to left).

3 Take the end (in this instance, from left to right) around the back of the standing part.

4 Tuck the end up through the loop to create the characteristic figure-of-eight layout.

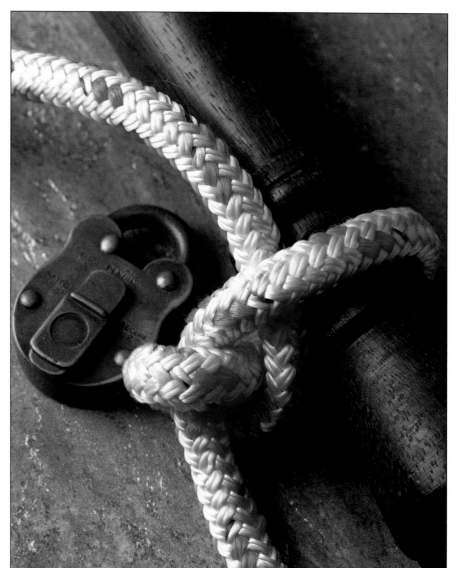

Highwayman's Hitch

Children like to learn and show off this hitch, because of the way its apparent complexity melts to nothing with one tug on the short end. Use it as a third hand for handiwork, as well as to moor or tether a boat or horse. There is no reason to believe that highwaymen ever actually used this knot.

1 Make a bight in one end of a rope, cord or other line and pass it up behind the hitching rail.

2 Pick up the standing part of the line and make a similar second bight at the front of the rail.

3 Tuck the second bight from front to back through the first one, then pull down on the working end to secure it.

4 Make a second bight in the working end (this is the third bight in total).

5 Tuck this third bight from front to back through the second one and finally pull down on the standing part to secure it. The final bight may be loaded; and the working end tugged for quick release.

Rolling Hitch

An elaboration of the clove hitch, this is intended to cope with a lengthwise pull. The two diagonal riding turns must go on the side of the object from which the pull will be applied.

1 Pass the working end around the anchorage from front to back.

2 Take the end up and diagonally across the front of the standing part.

3 Bring the working end down behind the work once more, bringing it out to emerge between the diagonal and the standing part.

4 Create a second diagonal turn, snugly beside the first one (and closest to the standing part), before passing the end down behind the work once more.

5 Tuck the working end up beneath the last diagonal turn only and lever it tight.

Ossel Hitch

"Ossel" is a Scottish sea fisherman's word (Cornish: "orsel") for a gill net. These knots secured the submerged lower ends of ossel lines that supported the nets as they were towed through choppy seas behind the fishing vessels known as drifters. Subjected to continual underwater movement, this seemingly simple knot coped with it all. It is a super little hitch.

1 Bring the working end down behind the foundation rope and around to the front.

2 Pass the end up and around the back of the standing part (in this instance, from left to right).

3 Take the working end down the front of the foundation rope and then bring it back up behind the work.

4 Finally, tuck the end over the first knot part and then beneath the second (as shown).

Ossel Knot

At the upper end of ossel ropes was this more secure knot which, in contrast to the submerged ossel hitch, had to resist being bashed about on the surface of rough seas.

1 Pass the working end up at the front, then over and down behind the foundation rope.

2 Bring the end up and diagonally across in front of the standing part and put it down behind the work.

3 Bring the working end up alongside the first wrapping turn and take it up for a second, diagonal wrapping turn.

4 Starting on the same side of the standing part, complete the second diagonal, so that it lies snugly beside the first one.

5 Wrap the working end up in front of the foundation rope once more, this time on the far side of the standing part from the two diagonal turns.

6 Pull out a loose bight in the standing part where it passes over the foundation rope.

7 Tuck the working end through the bight from front to back. Trap it by pulling down on the standing part.

Gaff Topsail Halyard Bend

A legacy from the days of wooden ships, oiled ropes and large canvas sails, even the name of this knot evokes an image of blustering storms and sea spray. However, this is a misleading name since this knot is actually a hitch, an oddity that comes from the fact that sailors, by some unwritten rule, always talked of "bending" ropes to rings or spars. It is sufficiently secure under a steady pull at right angles to the point of attachment.

1 Take the working end of the rope or other line up behind the rail or spar and then bring it down in front.

2 Pass the end up behind the anchorage once again, completing a turn.

3 Bring the working end down in front once more, making a full round turn, and take it behind its own standing part.

4 Finally tuck the end up (in this instance from left to right) beneath both parts of the round turn.

Vibration-proof Hitch

The American physicist Amory Bloch Lovins invented this knot over 20 years ago. It is designed for an anchorage of large diameter. Vibration of the standing part will only tighten it further due to the ratchet-like operation of the knot parts.

1 Pass the working end of the cord up, around and down the foundation from front to back, then take it diagonally up and to the right (in this instance) beneath its own standing part.

2 Take the end once more up, over and down behind the foundation.

3 Take the end across the front of the standing part then through the underlying diagonal (from left to right).

4 Go over the overlaying knot part and finally tuck the end beneath the diagonal again. Pull intermittently upon the standing part to tighten this knot.

Snuggle Hitch

This relatively new knot, which came to notice in 1987, was created by Owen K. Nuttall of West Yorkshire, England. Extra tucks and turns yield added security to withstand a variable pull in even synthetic cordage.

1 Take a turn with the working end and then leave it diagonally up and across the front of the standing part.

2 Pass the end down the back of the anchorage and bring it up at the front again.

3 Lead the working end across in front of the standing part to tuck it under its own previous pass.

4 Take the working end down behind the anchorage once again.

5 Lead the end over one knot part and tuck it beneath the next.

6 Take the working end down behind the work yet again, bringing it up at the front to go over one knot part and finally tuck beneath the next.

Boom Hitch

This attractive and robust hitch, described by Clifford Ashley in 1944, is quickly and easily tied with consecutive wrapping turns, and just a final single tuck to secure it. It really would, as the name suggests, cope with the variable direction and strength of pull involved as an improvised main sheet on a sailing dinghy, and it works equally well whether wet or dry.

1 Lay the working end diagonally up and across (in this instance, from left to right) the anchorage point.

2 Take the end down behind the anchorage and bring it under and forward again.

3 Lead the working end diagonally up and across its own standing part from right to left.

4 Take the end down again behind the anchorage and bring it forward.

5 Make a diagonal pass with the working end up and across from left to right over the intervening knot part.

6 Pass the end down behind the work between the two existing knot parts, to emerge at the front.

7 Take the end diagonally up from right to left over the standing end and one knot part.

8 Pass the working end down behind the anchorage to emerge at the front once again.

9 Make a final diagonal pass with the working end up from left to right, going over one knot part and tucking beneath the next. Make snug and tight.

Timber Hitch / Killick Hitch

The timber hitch is used by logging contractors to haul felled tree trunks from the undergrowth to the nearest transportation, although it will retrieve and drag all sorts of inanimate objects over rough terrain or through water.

For long and thin loads, such as scaffold poles or grounded flagmasts, an added half hitch (converting the initial timber hitch to a killick hitch) keeps them moving in a straight line. Because a "killick" was the naval name for a light anchor, rock or anything else that might hold a small boat on the sea or riverbed, a killick hitch was originally a rough-and-ready attachment for a boat, mooring buoy or even a lobster pot.

1 Pass the working end of a line up around the object to be towed and bring it to the front.

2 Take the end around its own standing part and make a small loop.

3 Tuck the working end through between the standing end and itself.

4 Bring the end around and repeat steps 2 – 3 to make a similar second tuck between the standing end and itself.

5 Complete the second tuck (adding a third and fourth if the diameter of the load and the cordage require the extra friction). Improvising a sliding noose in this way is known as "dogging".

6 Pull on the standing end to tighten the newly formed noose around the load. This is the basic timber hitch.

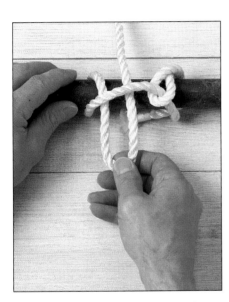

7 Make a half-hitch with the working end to convert a timber hitch into a killick hitch.

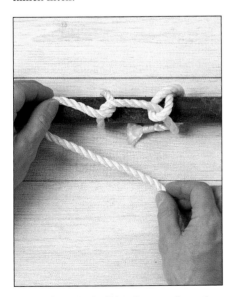

8 Locate the half-hitch away from the initial knot – perhaps a metre (about a yard) or more, depending on the scale of the job – to ensure a pull along the length of the load.

Clinging Clara

When the need arises to attach a thin line to a thicker rope for a lengthwise pull, this hitch really grips and holds. It is another creation by Harry Asher, dating from about 1989. The load must be applied to the standing part, which is on the right in the step pictures (taken upwards in the finished shot). Be prudent. Leave a longer working end than the one illustrated in the step-by-step tying shots.

1 Take a turn with the working end of the smaller line around the larger rope, in the direction of the strands if it is hawser-laid.

2 Bring the working end back towards the standing part of the thinner line.

3 Lead the working end across in front of the standing part, then around behind it, to return and pass over its own previous part.

4 Take the working end (in this instance, from right to left) over one knot part, finally tucking it beneath the initial turn.

Lighterman's Hitch

River Thames tugmen tow the Port of London's heavy dumb barges (lighters) with this strong, yet versatile hitch. It has also proved its worth with riggers in circus and theatre, as well as stevedores (longshoremen), being a heavy-duty professional holdfast that would support the weight of a massive marquee or berth an ocean liner. Yet, because this hitch never completely tightens, it is remarkably adaptable as it can be cast off effortlessly in seconds.

1 Pass the working end of the tow line or guy line around the post or peg.

2 Complete a round turn, using the friction gained to check or snub the load, and adjust the rope or other line to the required length.

3 Take hold of the working end (which must be fairly long) and pull out a bight from it.

4 Bring the bight beneath the taut standing part of the line and place it over the towing post, tent peg or other anchorage point.

5 Bring the working end over the top of the standing part, creating a small loop around it.

6 Take a turn around the post or peg with the working end.

Knute Hitch

This simple, and no doubt ancient, knot was named by American master rigger Brion Toss in 1990. It attaches a lanyard or halyard to anything with a small eye, so safeguarding objects such as pocket knives or other tools, securing a sail or fastening a curtain tie-back.

1 Make a small bight in the working end of the lanyard.

2 Push the bight through any hole that is barely bigger than the doubled cord.

3 Tuck the end (with a stopper knot added to it) through the bight and pull on the standing part to tighten.

Pile Hitch

Little known – and often not considered a "proper" knot – this simple hitch is tied more quickly than it can be described. It is ideal for attaching barrier ropes to posts and rails where the bight or loop can be passed over the top, for crowd control or to isolate road works. John Smith, an active member of the The International Guild of Knot Tyers, suggests that, if there were to be only one knot in the world, it would have to be this one – for it can (as he demonstrates) also be ingeniously adapted into a knot, bend, binding or loop.

1 Make a bight at any selected point in the rope or line.

2 Pass the bight beneath both standing parts, and loop it over the post, stanchion or peg. Both legs of the line may then be led in different directions.

Double Pile Hitch

John Smith devised this double pile hitch as an alternative to the rolling hitch to enable a lengthways pull.

1 Make a bight at any selected point in the rope or cord.

2 Pass the bight around the post, stanchion, peg or other item used as an anchorage point.

3 Take the bight beneath the two standing parts to make a turn.

4 Lead the bight further around the anchorage to complete a round turn.

5 Bring the bight beneath both standing parts and pass it over the anchorage. This hitch is designed to cope with a load from one or both of the standing parts and towards the bight.

Icicle Hitch

As an extension of his double pile hitch, John Smith first demonstrated this astonishng contrivance in May 1990 at the eighth Annual General Meeting of the International Guild of Knot Tyers, when he hung suspended by it from a splicing fid (tapered point down). As this demonstration proved, with careful arrangement this hitch will hold a considerable load on the smoothest of foundations – even a fireman's brass pole would be suitable. It has recently received fulsome praise from a civil engineer, who used it to lever a young tree out of the ground, after previous efforts by other means had failed and left the tree stripped of its bark and consequently slippery and smooth.

1 Lead the working end of the line over and around the foundation from front to back.

2 Take a round turn with the working end, working away from the direction of intended pull.

3 Create at least four turns, or more if an exceptionally secure hitch is required.

4 Drape the working end over the end of the foundation, as shown, with a bight hanging down at the back.

5 Bring the bight up in front of all the wrapping turns and both ends of the line, then pass it over the end of the foundation. Tighten everything by pulling each end in turn at right angles to the spar. Then tighten it again. Carefully apply the load, so that the knot stretches out (as illustrated). The final two turns – on the thicker part, if there is a taper – must not separate; if they do, add extra turns; once they remain together, the hitch should hold.

Bale Sling Hitch

This arrangement of an endless cargo strop will sling a sack, cask or any other load that is squat, round and inert. If a crane or other derrick is used, the upper bight would be put on to the hook with a cat's paw.

1 Lay the rope or webbing strop or sling beneath the load that is to be lifted.

2 Pass the bight that forms one end of the strop through the other end.

3 Pull up on the working bight to tighten the hitch; then simply release the load to loosen it again.

Ring Hitch

To attach any object – a knife, lucky mascot or other ornament – to a lanyard loop, use this hitch. If the loop is pre-tied in the lanyard, then it is obviously essential that the loop is long enough to pass over whatever is to be suspended from it.

1 Double a cord and pass the bight thus formed through the eye of the object to be attached.

2 Spread the bight wide enough to pass over the item on which it is being knotted.

3 Pull evenly upon both standing parts of the cord to tighten the hitch.

Cat's Paw

A strong hook or ring hitch for a heavy load, this strop hitch is used by stevedores (long-shoremen) in big hawsers and by anglers in considerably finer lines. Hanging double parts of loaded rope over a hook lessens the chance of it weakening. The cat's paw, when drawn up tightly, provides extra security. If, by chance, one leg of the rope should accidentally break, the other may take the weight of the load and enable the cargo to be lowered slowly to the ground, rather than allowing it to fall from a greater height.

1 Make a bight in an endless strop or double a length of line.

2 Bend the bight over to create a pair of matching loops.

3 Twist both loops, the lefthand one clockwise and the righthand in the opposite direction.

4 Continue until three or four twists have accumulated, with exactly the same number on each loop.

5 Insert the hook or other anchorage through both of the twisted loops.

6 Pull evenly on both standing parts to straighten them and slide the wrapping turns that result up snug to the hook or other fixture.

Anchor Bend

Related to the round turn and two half hitches, this even more secure hitch is used when a line is wet and slippery (such as one attached to the ring of a small boat's anchor). Because old-time sailormen "bent" a rope to an anchor or a spar, the hitches they used for this particular purpose acquired the contradictory and misleading name of "bends". This example is also known as the fisherman's bend.

1 Pass the working end of the line through the ring.

2 Lead the working end through the ring a second time, then bring it back to the standing part, completing a round turn.

3 Tuck the working end through the round turn and tie a half hitch.

4 Tie an identical second half hitch, leaving a longer end than illustrated. If a semi-permanent hitch is desirable, tape or tie it to the standing part of the line.

Anchor Bend Variant

This neat variant of the anchor bend was anonymously published back in 1904. It is effectively a round turn within a round turn, and it is snug, compact and secure.

1 Pass the working end of the line through the ring.

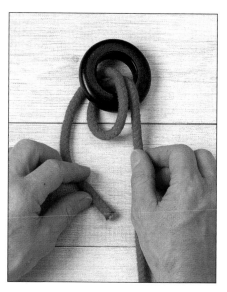

2 Lead the end through the ring a second time to create a round turn.

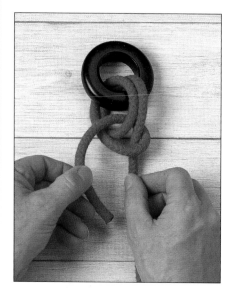

3 Tuck the working end through the round turn previously formed.

4 Then tuck the end a second time to create what is in effect one round turn through another round turn.

Halter Hitch

As with the highwayman's hitch, this knot is used, as its name implies, to tether animals. This is also a general-purpose hitch. Be warned, however, that some horses may chew on knots like this and ultimately undo them with their teeth.

1 Lead the working end through or around the anchorage point to cross its own standing part and form a loop.

2 Pass the end around and behind (in this instance, from left to right) to form a second loop beneath the first.

3 Make a bight in the working end and tuck it to tie a running overhand knot with drawloop.

4 Tighten the knot and adjust the sliding loop, then finish off by tucking the end through the drawloop to secure it.

Half Blood Knot

Anglers use this knot to attach a line to a hook, lure or swivel. Pull on the standing part of the line to convert the twists into snug wrapping turns.

1 Pass the working end through the ring that is the point of attachment.

2 Begin to twist the working end and the standing part together.

3 Continue the twisting process, ensuring an even tension on both parts of the line.

4 Make five or six twists, working away from the ring.

5 Bring the working end over and tuck it down through the loop, trapping it alongside the ring.

KNOTS

"He would lie in bed all morning . . .
practising knots with the cord he kept
by his bedside."
(MERVYN PEAKE – GORMENGHAST, 1950)

The word "knot" has a specific meaning,
apart from its general use for any cordage
entanglement. Strictly speaking, it refers
only to those that are not bends or hitches,
namely stopper knots, shortenings, loops and
bindings, as well as anything tied in string
or other small stuff, such as cotton or thread.
Stopper cordage knots may be used to prevent
fraying (when a whipping cannot be applied
immediately) but their function is primarily
to prevent the cord pulling out of a pulley-
block, fairlead or other opening. Shortenings
are temporary devices, intended
to avoid cutting rope that must later be reused.
Loops may be single or multiple, fixed or
sliding. Bindings can be makeshift quick
seizings or semi-permanent lashings,
while slide-and-grip knots are remarkable
shock-absorbing contrivances.

Ashley's Stopper Knot

The overhand knot, figure-of-eight knot and stevedore knot, despite their increasing bulks, will all pull through a hole of about the same diameter. For a fatter stopper, use this knot devised by Clifford Ashley sometime around 1910 after he had spied a lumpy knot, which he did not recognize, aboard a boat in the local oyster fishing fleet. This was the outcome, hence his name for it (the oysterman's stopper knot). Later, when he was able to see the mystery knot close up, it proved to be nothing but a wet and badly swollen figure-of-eight knot; but Ashley's new stopper knot has survived to become a minor classic.

1 Immobilizing the end, throw an overhand loop in the standing part of the line.

2 Take the standing part of the line beneath the loop.

3 Pull a bight through the loop to create an overhand knot with a drawloop.

4 Bring the working end up and through from the back of the bight (no other way will do). Pull the standing part down until the bight traps the end tightly against the knot.

Figure-of-Eight Knot

Favoured by dinghy sailors for the ends of jib leads and main sheets, this quick and simple knot has a bit more bulk than an overhand knot and is more easily untied – but it will escape through holes of roughly the same size. In its untightened form, this familiar knot has long been associated with faithful love – an emblem of interwoven affection.

1 Make a small bight at the end of the line and impart half a twist to turn it into a loop.

2 Impart an extra half twist to bring about the figure-of-eight shape that gives this knot its name.

3 Begin to pull the working end through the loop from the top. If you wish to leave a drawloop, stop at this stage.

4 Draw the working end right the way through to complete a common figure-of-eight knot. To tighten this knot, tug first on both ends to remove slack from the knot; then pull on just the standing part, pulling the end over and trapping it against the top of the knot.

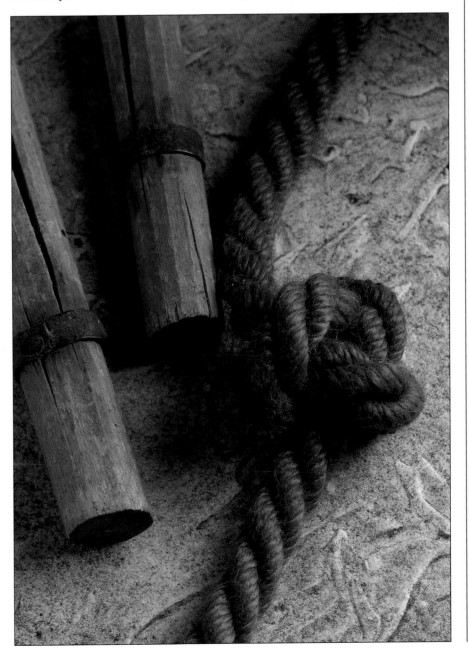

Stevedore's Knot

Prior to the advent of container craft, stevedores (longshoremen) worked aboard ships to load and unload cargoes piecemeal. Between them, they hoisted sacks, crates and casks in and out of warehouses by means of a rope through a single pulley, and this knot stopped it from coming free.

1 Make a small bight at one end of the line and give this bight half a twist to create a loop.

2 Add another half-twist to the bight to make interlocked elbows from the initial loop.

3 Add yet another half-twist, one beyond the making of a figure-of-eight knot.

4 Then, add a final half-twist (the fourth) to complete the preparation of this knot.

5 Tuck the working end up through the loop and carefully pull out all the slack, in this way encircling the standing part of the line and trapping the working end against the body of the knot with the bight.

Klemheist Knot

This knot may also be formed around a karabiner (not illustrated), which makes it easier to shift when prusiking.

1 Make a bight in part of an endless strop or sling.

2 Begin to wrap the sling upwards around the climbing rope.

3 Continue to create wrapping turns with the sling around the rope.

4 Ensure that both legs of the sling remain flat and parallel, with no crossovers, as the wrapping proceeds.

5 Complete four or five turns with the sling around the rope.

6 Tighten and neaten the wrapping turns (not perfectly illustrated) and bring the working bight down to the standing part of the sling.

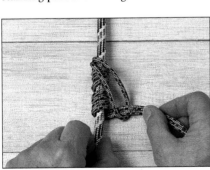

7 Tuck the remainder of the sling through the working bight to complete this friction hitch.

Mariner's Knot

To take the weight of a fallen climber off the belay device, a sling with a mariner's knot is attached to the anchors (and a klemheist to the climbing rope). The knot can be released under load, and works best with 1.4 cm/ $^7/_{12}$ in to 1.7 cm/$^7/_{10}$ in webbing. It is, presumably, named after its originator and has no nautical use.

1 Make a flattened bight in a webbing sling of appropriate width for the size of karabiner.

2 Pass the webbing bight over and through the appropriate karabiner.

3 Tuck the sling through the karabiner a second time to create a round turn.

4 Bring the working end of the sling around the front of the standing part.

5 Wrap it around the back of the standing part of the sling.

6 Wrap a second, third and fourth turn around the standing part.

7 Finally, tuck the working end of the sling between the two flat legs of the standing part. Friction and tension alone secure this hitch.

Penberthy Knot

Devised by Larry Penberthy and Dick Mitchell in about 1969, this prusiking knot is also known as the caver's helical knot. As it can be fiddly to tie, climbing writer Bill March suggests a sling weighted with a karabiner twirled around the rope, and the sling then threaded through it, makes tying much easier. Always adjust the number of turns and the amount of slack to the user's weight; too much slack and it slips, too little and it becomes difficult to shift.

1 Use a suitable size of accessory cord for the climbing rope.

2 Begin to wrap turns around the rope; it may not matter whether the turns go up (as illustrated) or down.

3 Wrap the accessory cord a second time around the climbing rope.

4 Continue until five or six wrapping turns have been completed.

5 Make an overhand loop in the upper one of the two cords.

6 Then take the lower cord and tuck it through this loop.

7 Take the working end (lower end of the cord) around the upper cord of the half-completed knot.

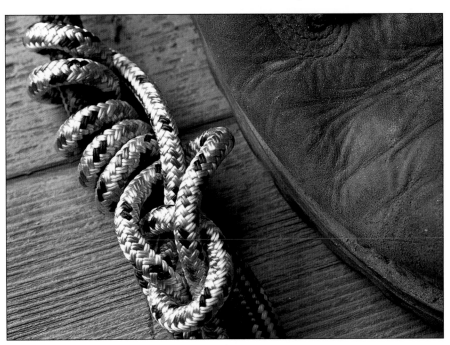

8 Tuck the end down through the loop to secure the arrangement with a sheet bend.

Munter Friction Hitch

An effective means of abseiling (rappelling), belaying or absorbing the energy of a fall, this friction hitch for kernmantel rope also reverses to yield slack or apply tension when needed. The rope is pressed around and through the karibiner and will break the fall of a climber by locking up, in much the same way that a car seat belt locks. Although it can be used for abseiling (rappelling), this is not generally recommended as the practice can be hard on the rope, eventually causing it to "burn". The munter friction hitch was introduced in 1974, and is also known as the Italian hitch and sliding ring hitch.

1 Use the climbing rope with an appropriate size and quality of karabiner.

2 Make a loop (exactly as illustrated) in the climbing rope.

3 Unscrew (if necessary) and open the gate of the karabiner.

4 Hook upwards with the karabiner to incorporate the climbing rope.

5 Then pass the karabiner through the initial loop from back to front (no other way will work).

6 When completed, this hitch is revealed as a dynamic crossing knot. The finished shot shows this knot from the rear side.

Double Munter Friction Hitch

Canadian rock and building climber Robert Chisnall devised and publicized this variation of the munter friction hitch. The additional turn around the karabiner creates greater friction and consequently more control over the load line. This is ideal for smaller diameter rope, which often needs more friction.

1 Choose an appropriate size and quality of karabiner to use with the climbing rope.

2 Make a double loop in the climbing rope, exactly as illustrated.

3 Hook upwards with the karabiner to incorporate the climbing rope.

4 Then pass the karabiner through the initial double loop from back to front as shown (no other way will work).

5 When completed, this hitch exerts more friction, and so will support greater loads than the basic knot.

Munter Mule

A rescuer's "extra hand", this contrivance may be a newcomer to the climbing scene. Ensure you try it out in training situations before resorting to it in trickier circumstances. Used for tying off an injured climber temporarily, this holdfast has the advantage that it can be untied while loaded. It is, in effect, a munter friction hitch – that dynamic relation of the inactive crossing knot – which has been immobilized by the addition of a slip knot backed up by an overhand knot (both tied in the bight). The munter mule's bulkiness makes it easy to undo.

1 Begin with a munter friction hitch tied on to a karabiner, and make a bight with the working end of the rope.

2 Pass the bight just made behind the standing part of the rope.

3 Bring the bight around to the front of the rope and tuck it down through its own loop.

4 Tighten the resulting overhand knot around the standing part of the rope. This is the munter mule.

5 Now take the working bight across the front of the rope, and return the bight around the back of the rope.

6 Finally tuck the working bight through its latest loop to reinforce it with a two-strand overhand knot around the standing part of the rope.

Release Hitch, Bottom Loaded

The bottom loaded version of this hitch, by contrast, is more secure than the prusik knot. It will grip even when sloppily tied, although it tends to drift apart when loaded if there is any slack. The trade-off is that the release end then has to be pulled very hard to make it slip. When tied neatly, the bottom loaded release hitch can be freed more easily.

1 Tie figure-of-eight loops in both ends of a length of accessory cord.

2 Arrange one end of the cord, knot down, alongside the climbing rope; then make an overhand loop as shown with the other end.

3 Lead the working end of the accessory cord around the back of the climbing rope.

4 Tuck the working end up through its earlier loop from front to back, and lead it around behind the rope.

5 Make the first of several wrapping turns to enclose both the cord and rope together.

6 Complete as many wrapping turns as necessary for the required friction.

7 Bring the working end out through the knot as shown and pull upon the unused end to tighten it.

Extended French Prusik Knot

This is another Robert Chisnall innovation from around 1981. It is a sort of Chinese finger trap, in which the extension brought about by a load reduces its diameter, so that it clings to the rope around which it is wrapped. To shift it by hand, grasp the upper end and pull down, thus shortening it and increasing its diameter, so that it releases its grip and slides. In fact, it is intentional that this knot slides under a shock loading as it absorbs energy until the falling load is low enough for the sling and rope to withstand, when it will grip and hold, thus making it ideal for climbers. This tape knot works equally well on a single or doubled climbing rope.

1 Middle a length of 25 mm/1 in tubular tape and arrange it with the bight around the climbing rope.

2 Lead both ends in opposite spirals around the rope, crossing one over the other when they meet.

3 Take both working lengths around to the back of the rope, where the one that went over at the previous crossing point now goes under.

4 Bring the tapes around to the front again, alternating the crossover once more.

5 Continue with this over-under-over wrapping of the tape around the rope.

6 Keep the diamond spaces between the tapes as small as possible.

7 Eight or ten wrapping turns are sufficient for this innovative knot.

8 Tie a pair of figure-of-eight loops as close to the rope as possible to be held by a karabiner.

Chi-Fi Knot

This variation of the extended French prusik knot, named after Canadian climbers Robert Chisnall and Jean-Marc Filion, is tied in an endless sling. It frees the user's hands for abseil (rappel) and rescue work. It is a close relation of the extended French prusik knot, also devised by Robert Chisnall. This clever slide-and-grip knot appeared first in the 1989 *Safety Manual* of the Ontario Rock Climbing Association, and may be unknown outside its membership. It is nevertheless a remarkable friction device that could prove useful in all kinds of situations. Aboard boats, the karabiner could be replaced by a shackle and pin. NOTE – This knot glazes slings, losing friction. Retire if glazing is apparent, and in any case after 10 to 12 uses in this way.

1 Place a tape sling around the climbing rope (which may be single or doubled), crossing one length of rope over the other.

2 Take both sections of tape around to the back of the rope, alternating the crossover.

3 Continue to wrap the tapes, with alternating crossovers, ensuring that the diamond spaces between the tapes are kept as small as possible.

4 Wrap the tapes until all of the slack in the sling is used up.

5 Neaten the lower half of the knot, until it matches the top half, and clip a karabiner through the two remaining bights.

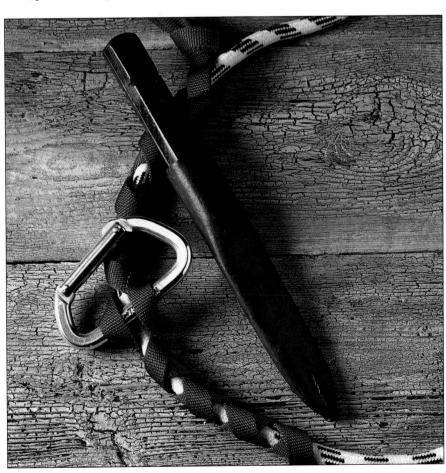

Square Knot

Dressing gown (bath robe) cords or other waist-ties may be fastened with this knot, allowing the ends to hang down stylishly. It is best, however, in a knotted scarf, when the four-panelled knot neatly fills the V-shaped space in an open blouse or shirt. Because there is already a square knot in the United States (which the British call the reef knot), Americans refer to this knot by several other names, including the rustler's knot, the Japanese crown knot, the Japanese success knot, the Chinese cross knot, and the Chinese good luck knot.

1 Make a bight in one of two cords, or one end of a single cord, and pass it around the other cord or end.

2 Lead the second cord up behind the initial bight in the other cord.

3 Bring the second cord down in front of the first one.

4 Pass the first working end over the front of the second to make a locking tuck through the open bight. Flatten and tighten this knot by pulling a bit at a time on each of the four strands that emerge from the knot.

Knife Lanyard Knot

Use this neat little knot to make a cord loop for a tool or to suspend an amulet or ornamental item from a necklace. It is a good-looking, versatile knot with a nautical pedigree.

1 Middle a length of cord, make a bight in one part of it and add a half-twist, as shown, to form a loop.

2 Lay the other part of the cord over the loop in the first part (in the direction shown).

3 Pass the second working end under the original standing part.

4 Then create a locking tuck that goes anticlockwise (counterclockwise) over-under-over-under to create a carrick bend with ends emerging on opposite sides of the knot.

5 Bring the upper, righthand end around anticlockwise (counterclockwise), over the standing part of the lefthand cord (under everything else) to tuck up through the centre opening.

6 Lead the bottom lefthand working end, similarly, anticlockwise (counterclockwise) over the standing part – but under everything else – to tuck up through the centre panel of the knot. Draw up with the utmost care, removing the slack a bit at a time, and ensuring that both standing parts go down together, while the working ends come up together.

Chinese Lanyard Knot

Less difficult to tie than it appears at first glance, the unusual square shape and texture of this knot make the result worth the effort. It can be used as a decorative means of holding two pieces of cord together – ideal for a necklace. Chinese knotting writer Lydia Chen calls this the plafond knot (*plafond* meaning decorated ceiling) because it resembles the motifs seen in Chinese temples and palaces.

1 Middle a length of cord and make a narrow bight in it.

2 Tie a half-knot with both ends of the cord length.

3 Tie an identical second half-knot to complete a loose granny knot.

4 Leave a gap of 7–8 cm/about 3 in and tie a second identical granny knot.

5 Invert the lower granny knot, turning it bottom-for-top.

6 Similarly invert the top granny knot, turning it top-for-bottom.

7 Tuck the original bight down through the centre of the lower granny knot.

8 Tuck the lefthand one of the two working ends up through the centre of the upper granny knot.

9 Turn the almost completed knot face down and bring the new lefthand working end out to the front.

10 Finally, tuck the lefthand working end up through the upper granny knot. Ensure that the loop is long enough to go over the object it will hold, then patiently remove the slack from this knot (slowly does it), working towards both working ends.

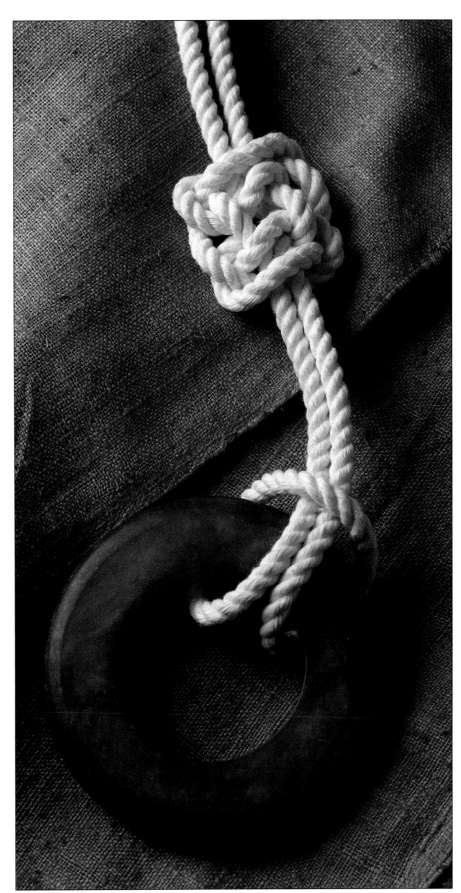

Good Luck Knot

For a robust knot, easy to tie and tighten, this has a striking finished appearance. Use it for gift-wrapped parcels or simply hang it from a belt as a novel chatelaine for keys (keychain). The appearance of this knot will be enhanced if, between the three large loops, the four small ones are left open.

1 Middle a single length of cord and make a narrow bight in it.

2 Pull out and retain a second bight in the lefthand leg of the cord.

3 Pull out a matching bight in the righthand leg of the cord.

4 Lay both standing parts of the cord up and over the lefthand bight.

5 Take the lefthand bight and lay it over the upper bight.

6 Take the upper bight and lay it down over the righthand bight.

7 Tuck the righthand bight over and through beneath the two standing parts of the cord.

8 Without distorting it in any way, carefully tighten the resulting four-part crown knot.

9 Bring the lefthand bight down and cross the lower bight up over it.

10 Lay the righthand bight up and over the lower bight.

11 Lead the two standing parts of the cord down in a final locking tuck through the vacant bight. Tighten the second crown knot atop the first one.

Chinese Button Knot

This is a classic button knot that can be stitched to a bag or purse and serves either as an attractive fastening or a decorative accessory. Knotted buttons tend to be too large for buttonholes, so fasten them with cord loops or frogs. Tied with craft and patience in very small fine material, button knots make unusual earrings. In some stiff materials, this knot can be made to stay flat, for ornamentation rather than practicality.

1 Middle – more or less – a short length of decorative cord.

2 With one end of the cord make an overhand loop.

3 Then pass the working end down behind the loop just formed.

4 Pick up the other end and tuck it (in this instance, from left to right) under-over-under-over; keep hold of the partially formed knot, as this is not a locking tuck.

5 Finally lead the later working end up and down through the knot as shown.

Prise up as knot tightens

6 Arrange the four-lobed symmetrical knot with the two standing cord parts as a stem, then gradually remove the slack until the knot becomes convex like a mushroom. As it tightens, the central knot part (indicated in the illustration) will tend to recede from sight and must be prised up to the surface of the knot where it will then remain.

Chinese Button Knot (Doubled)

The Chinese button knot is often doubled to produce a bulkier and therefore showier knot. When making this version, it is not necessary to prise up the top central part, which is supported by underlying strands.

1 Continue from step 6 of the Chinese button knot and bring the two working ends alongside one another.

2 Begin to follow the original lead with one of them.

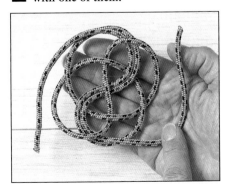

3 Using the other end, start to follow the original lead around in the opposite direction.

4 Continue with both ends until the single-ply knot is entirely doubled.

5 Tuck the ends down through the centre of the knot and carefully tighten it.

Wrapped & Reef Knotted Coil

Rope coiled this way and secured with reef (square) knots has a good chance of surviving any journey tangle-free. This is a quick and simple arrangement that serves to prevent all sorts of frustrating entanglements. It works for thick rope and smaller cordage, and is easy to untie when the rope is required.

1 Bring the two ends of the coiled rope close together, and tie a half-knot (with longer ends than are illustrated).

2 Then add a second half-knot (of opposite handedness) to complete a reef (square) knot.

3 Wrap both ends away from the reef (square) knot, with identical helixes, so as to secure the coil.

4 Where the two ends meet opposite the original reef (square) knot, tie another half-knot.

5 Then add a second half-knot (of opposite handedness) to complete a second reef (square) knot.

Alpine Coil

This is the method of securing a coil of rope for transport that is traditionally preferred by climbers and cavers.

1 Bring the two ends of the coiled rope close together.

2 Bend one end back to create a bight about 15–20 cm/6–8 in long.

3 Wrap the other end around the coiled rope, including the bight.

4 Ensure that the second wrapping turn traps and holds the initial turn.

5 Wrap fairly tightly and keep each succeeding turn snug.

6 Complete at least six wrapping turns, then tuck the working end through the bight (pulling upon the other end to secure it).

Figure-of-Eight Coil

This is the storekeeper's way of hanging coils up out of harm's way. Coiling the rope double is the trick that makes this coil fast and effective, with a practical loop to hang it by. Ropes travelling in the back of a car can always be coiled this way as they can be held in place by securing the loop around a fixed object. It is, like many of the coils, quick and easy to untie, if required in an emergency.

1 Middle the rope prior to coiling and then coil it doubled.

2 Bring the bight back upon itself so as to create a loop.

3 Lead the working bight around the back of the coil to the other side.

4 Finally tuck it up through its own loop (and the entire coil), from front to back, to make a loop from which to hang it.

Fireman's Coil

This method of forming a coil with a useful hanging loop is probably the most basic coil and deserves to be better known.

1 Bring the two ends of the coiled rope close together.

2 With one of the ends, make an overhand small loop.

3 Pass the working end through the coil and behind it, and make a bight.

4 Tuck the bight up through the loop, from behind, and gently pull it tight. Suspend the coil from this loop.

Grief Knot

Combining the characteristic failings of both granny and thief knots, this is the most insecure of knots, diagonally unbalanced and with an uneven pull from short ends on opposite sides. But there is a trick to it. Pull both ends and gently roll the knot to tighten it; then lever them on to opposite sides so that they lock solid. In this way the knot can be used to bind together garden trelliswork and similar lightweight structures.

1 Make a small bight in one end of the cord or line.

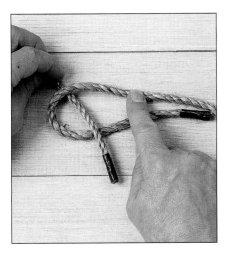

2 Tuck the working end up through the bight, angling it towards the other short end.

3 Now tuck the working end under the first part of the bight but then over the standing part of the bight.

4 Finally, return the working end back through the bight to emerge from the completed knot alongside its own standing part.

Pole Lashing

A pair of these lashings, plus a couple of reef (square) knots, will seize and subdue an armful of metal tent-poles or any awkward assortment of long and thin objects.

1 Arrange the cord in an "S" or "Z" shape beneath and close to one end of the objects to be tied up.

2 Tuck one end down through the bight on the opposite side to it.

3 Bring the other end across and tuck it in its turn down through the remaining bight.

4 Pull up both working ends, so that the bights snugly embrace the enclosed objects.

5 Cross the two ends (left over right in this instance), tying the first half of a reef (square) knot, and pulling it tight.

6 Bring the ends back together (right over left) and complete the reef (square) knot. With a second length of cord, repeat steps 1 to 6 at the other end of the objects.

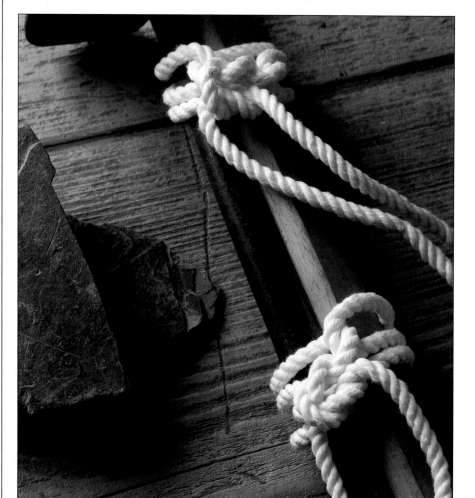

Bag Knot

Like other such knots – which also go under the generic name of sack knots – this dates from the days when grain and other granular or powdered materials were bagged up in sacks, the necks of which were then tied with practised familiarity by millers and grain merchants. Leave a drawloop (as shown) for easy release later if necessary.

1 Wrap the working end of a short length of cord around the neck of the bag or sack.

2 Bring the end up to the left, crossing over itself in the process.

3 Lead the end down behind the bag and then up at the front.

4 Now take the working end across to the right once more, and double it to make a small bight.

5 Finally, tuck the bight to serve as a drawloop, working the completed knot snug and tight.

Sack/Miller's Knot

Unlike the bag knot, the sack knot, which is a binding from an earlier age, cannot be tied in the bight, but it is another one in which a drawloop may be left to prevent possible damage to the bag if the knot is cut.

1 Drape a short length of cord around the neck of the bag or sack with the short end hanging down in front of the bag.

2 Move the short end at the front over to the left.

3 Wrap the longer working end up and over the neck of the bag or sack, from front to back, taking care to trap the short end in place.

4 Take the working end down around the back of the bag and bring it up at the front again.

5 Tuck the end down through the space retained between the first and second wrapping turns and pull it snug and tight. Leave a drawloop, if preferred.

Constrictor Knot, Tied with an End

An alternative to the strangle knot, the constrictor knot can be the best of binding knots. Use it with or without a drawloop as a semi-permanent seizing on rope's ends, hose-pipes, and for every odd job imaginable. The ancient Greeks may have used it for surgical slings, and it could well be the "gunner's knot" that in later centuries seized the necks of flannel-bag gunpowder cartridges for muzzle-loading artillery. It was re-discovered and popularized by Clifford Ashley in 1944. Use this tying method when the end of the foundation rope, spar or whatever, is not easily accessible. To remove a constrictor – without nicking or scarring whatever lies beneath it – carefully sever the overriding diagonal with a sharp knife, when the knot will drop off in two curly cut segments.

1 Take a short length of cord or twine (hard-laid to bind softer objects, such as rope; soft and stretchy for unyielding foundations) and arrange it around whatever is to be tied.

2 Bring the working end of the binding cord up and across to the right over its own standing part.

3 Lead the end down at the back and up once more at the front.

4 Tuck the working end beneath the diagonal made earlier, completing a clove hitch.

5 Locate and loosen the upper lefthand knot part, preparatory to tucking in the working end.

6 Bring the working end across and tuck it from left to right through the loosened bight. Pull both ends in opposite directions to tighten this knot as hard as possible, when the ends may be cut off quite close to the knot.

159

Constrictor Knot, Tied in the Bight

This is another example of the excellent constrictor knot. Tie it more quickly this way when the end of the foundation rope, spar, or whatever, is accessible. When pulled tight it will lock securely. With practice, a constrictor knot tied by this method can be applied quicker than the eye can follow the actions.

1 Lead the working end of a short length of cord or twine, from front to back, over the object to be seized.

2 Lift the working end so as to complete a full turn.

3 Pull a fairly long bight down from the lower part of the turn just made.

4 Lift the bight and half-twist it (as shown) to place it over the end of the foundation.

5 Heave on both ends, as strongly as the cord or twine will withstand, to tighten the knot; then cut off the ends close to the knot.

Transom Knot

Clifford Ashley originally made this knot to seize together two cross-sticks for his daughter's kite. It is an adaptation of the constrictor knot and can be used for any light trelliswork. If greater strength is needed, add a second knot facing the first one and at right angles to it.

1 The components to be lashed with this knot need to be at right angles.

2 Lead the working end over the horizontal uppermost element of the construction and around the back of the vertical piece.

3 Bring the end diagonally down and across over its own standing part.

4 Now lead it around the back of the vertical piece beneath the horizonal section and return it to the front of the work once more.

5 Tuck the end through beneath the diagonal knot part, so as to form a half-knot with the two opposing cord ends. Pull as tight as possible.

Double Constrictor Knot

This variation of the constrictor knot has extra internal friction and grip; it is also more suitable for binding objects with a larger diameter, or when the objects are an awkward shape and will not automatically pull together. When tying a particularly awkward package and hands are not enough to tighten this seizing as much as required, attach each end of the cord to a screwdriver or similar handle by means of a pile hitch to apply extra leverage.

1 Wrap the cord around the item to be secured. Bring the working end diagonally up and take it across over its own standing part.

2 Lead the working end down behind the work and then up in front once more, taking care to keep between the standing part and the initial turn.

3 Take the working end up and around the foundation again, doubling the characteristic diagonal that overlays the single version of this knot.

4 Put the working end directly down behind, to emerge at the front (on the righthand side of its standing part).

5 Tuck the end through the two turns so it is parallel and to the right of its own standing part.

6 Locate and loosen the upper lefthand part of this almost completed knot, preparatory to the final tuck.

7 Bring the working end across and tuck it from left to right through the loosened bight.

8 Pull the knot as tight as possible and cut the ends off close to the knot.

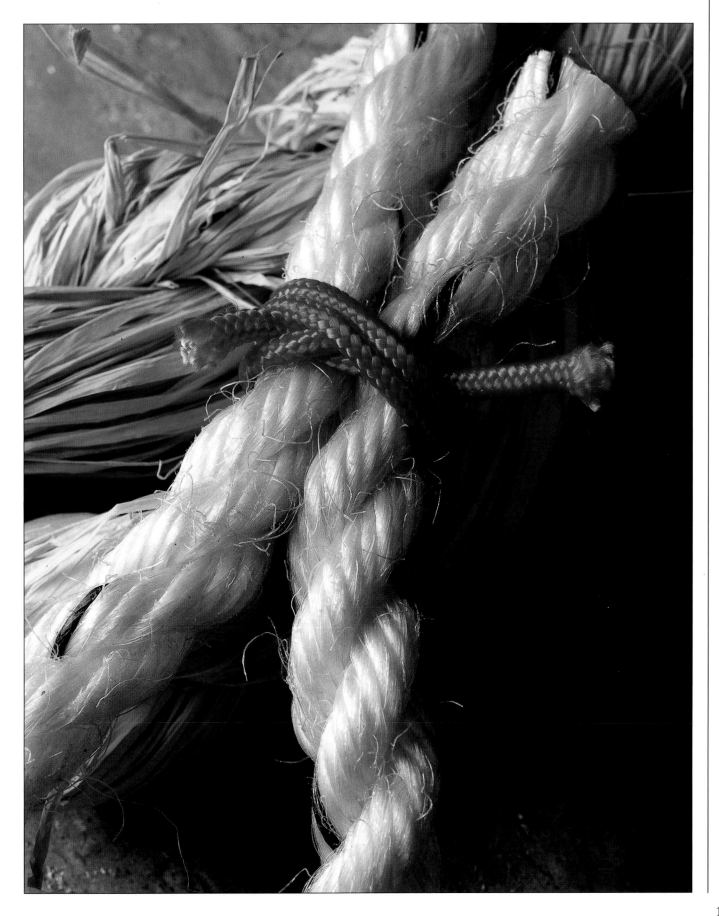

Boa Knot

This robust binding was devised and announced in 1996 by the accomplished weaver Peter Collingwood, who wanted a knot that would remain securely in place when the foundation around which it was tied was cut close alongside the knot. It combines the structures and qualities of both strangle and double constrictor knots, a really secure arrangement; yet it is quick and easy to tie, and this has ensured its prompt adoption by many discerning knot tyers.

1 Make an overhand loop with a short length of the chosen material.

2 Add a similar second turn on top of the first one.

3 Arrange these turns in the form of a coil with both ends lying in the same direction; there should be three cord parts under each thumb.

4 Rotate the righthand side of this coil through 180°, as shown (that is, to put the bottom where the top had been).

5 Check that the resulting figure-of-eight has three knot parts around each loop and in the overlaying diagonal, with just two parts underneath.

6 Begin to insert the rope, rod or whatever is to be seized, beneath one or other of the end loops.

7 Continue by sliding the foundation over the centre crossing, which totals five knot parts.

8 Push it carefully through the far loop, when the knot will be completely held upon it.

9 Finally, work this knot snugly into shape, with three twined knot parts overlaid by a pair of diagonals. The ends may be cut much shorter than shown.

Jug, Jar or Bottle Sling

The interwoven knot parts of this clever contrivance will cling unyieldingly to the narrow neck of a bottle, providing it has a very slight, narrow lip, or provide substantial carrying handles for a larger jug or jar (pitcher) – even an ancient Greek amphora. Use it to cool picnic wine in a mountain stream, to lug a churn of milk across the farmyard or to suspend a hanging basket of flowers from a kitchen beam.

1 Roughly middle an appropriate length of strong cord and make a long bight.

2 Bend the bight down to create two matching long loops.

3 Overlap the two loops of cord by laying the righthand one upon the lefthand one.

4 Locate the section of cord that overlays both legs of the original bight and begin to pull it up beneath the existing layout.

5 Pull out a bight and make a locking tuck with it over-and-under through the overlapped loops.

6 Extend the working bight about 7 cm/2¾ in beyond the half-completed knot.

7 Take hold of the large curving loop at the back of the knot.

8 Then pull it down to touch the two standing parts of the cord.

9 Take hold of the similar large curving loop at the front of the knot.

10 Pull this loop down too until it touches the two standing parts of the cord.

11 Tug gently and experimentally on both bight and cord legs until the tension is evenly distributed throughout the resulting braided bracelet of a knot.

12 Place the knot around the neck of the chosen jug (pitcher), jar or bottle and pull the outer loops as tight as possible.

13 Insert one of the long ends through the shorter loop, then tie the two ends together with a fisherman's knot or other secure bend, to create two self-adjusting handles that will always be the same length when held.

Asher's Equalizer

This cunning knot, added to a jug (pitcher), jar or bottle sling, adjusts loop lengths automatically to give two handles the same size, which makes carrying the object much easier. It was devised by Harry Asher in the mid-1980s.

1 Ensure the completed jug (pitcher), jar or bottle sling has two long ends and a shorter loop.

2 Start to pull the two long ends a short way through the loop until they create twin bights.

3 Bring the single large loop formed by the knotted ends over the twin bights just formed.

4 Pull the twin bights completely through the single large loop.

5 Tighten the resulting knot to create a pair of matching handles.

Double Figure-of-Eight Hitch

Owen K. Nuttall came across this knot as a forerunner to his snuggle hitch; but it is arguably an even better binding knot. The attraction of this particular form is the easily acquired and memorized double figure-of-eight layout. Try it as an alternative to the boa and constrictor knots.

1 First make a clockwise overhand loop with one end of a length of cord or twine.

2 Add an anticlockwise (counterclockwise) overhand loop to form a figure-of-eight.

3 Lay a second clockwise overhand loop on top of the first one.

4 Pick up the other end and place another clockwise overhand loop atop the remaining single loop.

5 Begin to slide the knot over its intended core, or insert the core through the knot, as shown.

6 Locate the knot where required on and around the object to be seized.

7 Pull on both ends as hard as possible to tighten this binding knot.

Square Turk's Head (4 Lead x 5 Bight)

This Turk's head knot has four interwoven strands (or leads) with five scallop-shaped rim parts (bights). These dimensions give it a shorthand label: it is known as a 4-lead x 5-bight Turk's head (abbreviated further when written to 4L x 5B TH). All Turk's heads that have just one lead more or less than the number of bights are also referred to as "square" Turk's heads. This tying method was developed by Charlie Smith.

1 Middle a length of cord and lead the working end around the base of the thumb, over the standing part, to go (from front to back) between the first and second fingers.

2 Take the end around the forefinger, then up through (under-and-over) the thumb loop, and beneath the standing part.

3 Now lead the working end between the second and third fingers, and around the second finger, to tuck under one/over two/under one (as illustrated).

4 Pass the end over the standing part and between the third and little fingers, returning between the second and third fingers and tucking up through the second finger loop.

5 Lead the working end, in a final satisfactory locking tuck, over/under/over/under/over, and then tuck the end up alongside the standing part, as shown.

6 The completed knot may remain flattened, or be turned into a bracelet, and (in form) doubled or tripled by following the original lead around with the surplus cord of the unused standing end. The main picture shows a tripled bracelet.

Square Turk's Head (5 Lead x 4 Bight)

Use this single-strand Turk's head instead of one or other of the common whippings to seize the cut ends of ropes. A square Turk's head like this makes a pretty but practical sliding sleeve for the drawcord on a duffel bag. Then again, it can embellish anything it will fit, from bellropes and handrails to key fobs or the gear shift of a classic sports car.

1 Middle a length of cord and pass the working end over and down behind the core, to reappear on the right of the standing part. Go diagonally up (from right to left) over the previous lead.

2 Take the end over, around and down behind the core, emerging to the immediate right of the standing part, tucking over one/under one/ over one, from right to left.

3 Lead the working end down behind the core, to reappear again just to the right of the standing part, and tuck (left to right) under one/over one.

4 Rotate the work, bringing the rear side into view, and tuck the end (right to left) over/under/over.

5 Turn the work back to its original position and tuck the working end to the right of the standing part (and left to right) over/under/over.

6 Rotate the work, to show the rear side. Lead the end (right to left) in a final locking tuck under/over/under/over.

7 Place the working end alongside the standing part to complete the knot, which may then be doubled and tripled by following around the original lead with the surplus cord.

Twined Turk's Head (2 Lead x 3 Bight)

This primitive version of a Turk's head is unusual. It is rarely seen, although it has been used to bind the ends of hunting crops.

1 Tie an overhand knot around the chosen core with the working end of a length of cord.

2 Lead the end over, around and down behind the core, to reappear to the right of the standing part.

3 Tuck the working end alongside the standing part and parallel to it.

4 Follow the original lead with the working end, tucking under and staying parallel to it (on the same side).

5 Continue to reproduce the original lead, doubling the knot with the working end.

6 Tuck the working end under the next loop, following the standing part as before.

7 Tuck the working end in to complete. Make a 2L x 3B TH this way. With an initial double overhand knot, produce a 2L x 5B TH. A treble overhand knot results in a 2L x 7B TH. A quadruple overhand knot creates a 2L x 9B TH, and so on.

Spade End Knot

Anglers attach monofilament to spade-ended (eyeless) hooks, or short leader lengths to thicker lines, with this knot. It is akin to perfected whipping.

1 Make a loop in the thinner stuff and arrange it so that the short end is alongside the thicker line.

2 Leaving the short end in position, begin to wrap the body of the loop, enclosing and holding both parts of itself as well as the thicker line.

3 Continue to bind tightly, with each succeeding turn snugly up against the preceding one.

4 Complete about 2 cm/⅝ in of wrapping, then pass the shrunken loop over the end of the thicker line.

5 Remove any remaining slack from the bight, then pull in opposite directions on both ends to tighten.

LOOPS

"A hemp noose rough on the sunburned skin of the neck . . ."
(DOUGLAS BOTTING – *THE PIRATES*, 1979)

The hangman's noose, brandished by every Hollywood lynch mob, is a splendid example of a secure and strong knot designed to absorb a shock loading without breaking the rope. It is just one of the family of blood or barrel-shaped knots, with several wrapping turns, utitilized in their own specialized materials by anglers, cavers and climbers, veterinarians and surgeons – but not, in fact, by many public executioners. They preferred a simple reinforced eye with the standing part of the rope passing freely through it. A loop knot may be used like a hitch, but placed over a post or rail (rather than tied around it), the advantage being that it is easily removed again for re-use. Double and multiple loops are for improvised working hoists and rescue slings (in the absence of better alternatives). Running knots or nooses, useful for parcels, may have originated as snares to catch animals and birds for food. Some loops are tied in the bight, others in the end of cordage.

CAUTION

A growing body of legislation discourages the use of makeshift loop knots, and improvised slings, in favour of properly manufactured and tested safety harnesses and rigging. Nevertheless, there will always be situations when – to save life – it might still be acceptable to grab a coil of rope and put together a rescue knot or two. At those times, one or other of the following knots would still be justified.

Angler's Loop

This is an old angling knot, from the 17th-century days of Sir Izaak Walton and lines made of gut, which has resurfaced as a secure loop knot for the latest manmade ropes. It will even stay tied in bungee (elasticated) shock cord. This knot too can be tied in the bight, but the method illustrated is easier to learn and remember.

1 Immobilize the end of the line and make an overhand loop with the standing part.

2 Bring the end over and lay it across the initial loop.

3 Pull a bight through to create what is, at this stage, an overhand knot with a drawloop.

4 Lead the working end around behind the standing part of the line.

5 Tuck the end through the centre of the knot, trapping it neatly beneath the two legs of the loop.

Figure-of-Eight Loop

Referred to by sailormen once upon a time as a Flemish loop, the figure-of-eight loop was viewed by them with disfavour because it tended to jam in wet hemp or manilla ropes and could not easily be untied after loading. Cavers and climbers now prefer this versatile alternative to the bowline. It is easily tied – even by an uncertain beginner – and readily checked by a team leader (in the poorest light and the worst weather). Tie the working end to the standing part for added security.

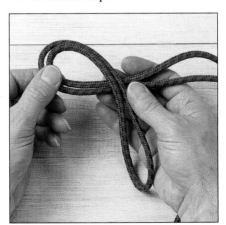

1 Make a generous bight in the end of the cord or rope.

2 Impart half a twist in the bight to create twin loops, as shown.

3 Add an extra half-twist to the loops already produced, as shown.

4 Tuck the bight through the twin loops and work the completed knot neatly snug and tight.

Bowline

Once this knot was used for attaching a line from the bow of a ship to the weather leech of a square-sail, holding it closer to the wind, and thus preventing it being taken aback (blown inside out). Nowadays the same bowline (pronounced "boh-linn") is used, misused and abused for innumerable other jobs from tying parcels to tree surgery. Among its advantages are that it does not slip, loosen or jam. It remains a time-honoured knot, which may, however, need to have its working end tied or taped to the adjacent loop leg for added security.

1 Bring the working end across the standing part of the rope to form an overhand loop.

2 Rotate the hand clockwise and so produce a smaller loop in the standing part of the rope.

3 Ensure that the working end points upwards (from back to front) through the small loop.

4 Lead the end around behind the standing part of the rope.

5 Then tuck it back down through the small loop, this time from front to back.

6 Arrange the completed knot with a long end (longer than shown) and consider further securing it with tape, a half hitch or other extra fastening.

Eskimo Bowline

This variation on the orthodox bowline is sometimes referred to as the Boas bowline. The Arctic explorer Sir John Ross (1777–1856) brought an Inuit (Eskimo) sled back to England that had been presented to him by Inuits. It contained numerous such knots in its rawhide lashings, evidence that this was a genuine Inuit knot. The sled is now in the basement of the Museum of Mankind, London. As it is more secure than the common bowline, especially in synthetic lines, it is worth learning.

1 Make an underhand loop in one end of the rope.

2 Bring the standing end down behind the loop, creating an incomplete overhand knot.

3 Lift the standing part of the rope up slightly within the loop.

4 Then make a locking tuck (over/under/over) with the working end of the rope.

5 Let the working end be pulled into a bight by the marlinespike hitch.

6 Draw the marlinespike hitch down over the bight. Note the untypical face of this bowline, when tightened, with its distinctive trefoil crown.

Double Bowline

With the reinforced nip, this knot is stronger (70 to 75 per cent) and more secure than the common bowline. With a fairly long end, it may not need to be taped or tied.

1 Make an anticlockwise (counter-clockwise) overhand loop.

2 Add another identical loop above (or behind) the first one.

3 Bring the two loops together, preparatory to tucking the working end through them.

4 Tuck the end up through the combined loops from behind.

5 Lead the working end around behind the standing part of the rope.

6 Then tuck it down through the double loop, beside its own other part, with a moderately long tail end.

Bimini Twist

This remarkably strong loop (95–100 per cent), recommended for big game fishing, has been in print since at least 1975. It is illustrated for clarity in much larger cordage than would in fact be used; consequently, it was not possible to show realistically how the hands – and feet – would actually cooperate in tying this knot with fine monofilament or braid. Still, the various stages are correctly shown. The numerous initial twists, simply imparted with a forefinger, are then spread apart to create the overlaying series of wrapping turns that strengthen and finish off this knot.

1 Make a bight over 50 cm/20 in long. Insert a finger in the end of the bight and begin to twist a loop around.

2 Impart some 20 twists to the bight, holding both parts of the line so that they do not unwind.

3 Spread the loop. In practice, this must be done with the feet, while both hands are free to control the two upper ends of the line. Start to enlarge the loop to unwind the initial twists.

4 An overriding layer of wrapping turns should appear where the hands are focused. Hold the standing part taut and feed the working end at right angles into these turns under steady tension, keeping them tight and close together.

5 With the working end, take a half hitch around one leg of the large loop.

6 Finally, make a half hitch with the working end around both legs of the loop.

Portuguese Bowline

Old-time sailormen were a polyglot tribe who shipped aboard any vessel that would have them, so knot names spread haphazardly. Felix Reisenberg called this a French bowline; whereas Clifford Ashley, who spotted it aboard Portuguese boats in his home town of New Bedford, Massachusetts, gave it the current name. It was used as a kind of boatswain's chair, with the crewman's legs through one loop and his back supported by the other one.

1 Form a small overhand loop with the working end of the rope.

2 Make a large loop in the same direction and of roughly the required working size.

3 As the working end approaches the smaller loop, take it behind.

4 Bring it up and through the cinch as if tying a common bowline.

5 Take the end around the back of the standing part of the rope.

6 Finally, tuck the end down through the cinch and tighten the resulting knot around the two trapped loop parts. Ensure the end is longer than illustrated.

Portuguese Bowline with Splayed Loops

A couple of these versatile knots will sling a plank or ladder as an improvised work platform, but note that each one of the two loops can pull slack from the other. Do not use this knot in circumstances where this may prove an undesirable feature. An illustration of this knot appeared in *Tratado de Apparelho do Navio*, (1896), Lisbon, and Clifford Ashley reports having first seen it used aboard Portuguese ships.

1 Arrange the line as shown in the illustration above.

2 Reduce the size of the lower loop, secure the lefthand bight, and bring the working end around to create a second loop on the righthand side of the emerging knot.

3 Tuck the working end up through the small central loop and then take the end around behind the standing part of the rope.

4 Finally, tuck the end down through the central loop or cinch. Adjust the two working loops to the required size, and then begin to tighten the familiar bowline layout.

Tom Fool's Knot

This is one of many so-called handcuff knots that, according to knot lore, can render any Houdini helpless. In fact, they were probably used for hobbling farm animals overnight, as an alternative to a picket line, so as to leave them free to graze. Tie this knot in the bight.

1 Cast a clockwise overhand loop, tying it in the bight of the chosen rope or cord.

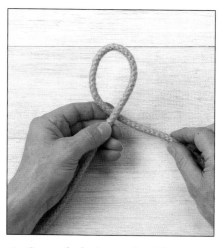

2 Add an anticlockwise (counterclockwise) underhand loop, of similar size to the first one.

3 Partly overlap the two loops, the lefthand one in front of the righthand one, and prepare to pull the leading edge of the lefthand loop (from the front to the back) through the righthand loop, at the same time pulling the leading edge of the righthand loop (from the back to the front) through the lefthand loop.

4 Pull out twin loops, adjust them to the required size, then tighten the knot.

Handcuff Knot

This takes a second or so more to tie than the simple Tom Fool's knot since the twin loops are interlocked, but it is doubtful that this more elaborate version is stronger or more stable than the simpler knot.

1 Cast a clockwise overhand loop, tying it in the bight of the rope.

2 Add a second loop, anticlockwise (counterclockwise) and underhand.

3 Partly overlap the loops, with the righthand one coming in front of the lefthand one.

4 Pull the leading edge of the lefthand loop (from the back to the front) through the righthand loop; at the same time pull the leading edge of the righthand loop (from the front to the back) through the lefthand loop.

5 Adjust the loops to the required size and then tighten the knot.

Fireman's Chair Knot

Either the handcuff knot or the Tom Fool's knot is the basis for this. Colin Grundy, who studied the fireman's chair knot, reported that either worked well. One loop, adjusted for size, fits beneath the subject's armpits, with the other loop around behind the knees. A rescuer then lowers the person by means of one long end, while a second rescuer pulls them away from the wall, cliff or other hazard with the lower rope.

1 Cast a clockwise overhand loop in the bight of the rescue rope.

2 Then add an anticlockwise (counterclockwise) underhand loop of similar size to the first one.

3 Partly overlap both loops, ensuring that the righthand one is in front of the left.

4 Pull the leading edge of the lefthand loop (from the back to the front) through the righthand loop; at the same time pull the leading edge of the righthand loop (from the front to the back) through the lefthand loop.

5 Pull on both loops at once to tighten the knot so far formed.

6 Take the lefthand standing part around the back of the lefthand loop and bring it over to the front.

7 Take the working end down through its own loop to tie a half hitch.

8 Take the righthand standing part over the top of the righthand loop and round the back.

9 Tuck the working end through its own loop from back to front to tie another half hitch.

7 Lead the working end once around the almost completed parcel, prior to tucking it beneath itself.

8 Finally, dog the working end around its own standing part to secure.

Diamond Hitch

Explorers, prospectors and other wilderness pioneers, dependent upon pack animals to convey all sorts of loads, once swore by this hitch, and it can still be spotted in the more authentic cowboy films. The lashing will secure irregularly shaped commodities, as they stir and strain, not only on the backs of mules and horses but also loaded on to beach buggies, snowmobiles or other motor vehicles (on or off-road). It is also ideal for human backpackers with unpackable items to carry.

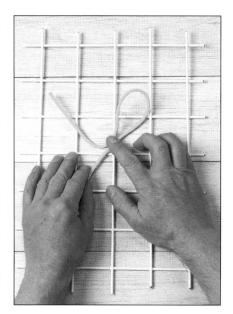

1 Select a suitable length of lashing for backpack or luggage rack.

2 Secure the standing end to a centrally placed anchorage point.

3 Take the line loosely across the load, around a second anchorage opposite the first, then return.

4 Twist the two parts of the lashing together, until most of the slack is removed. Find the centre of the twist.

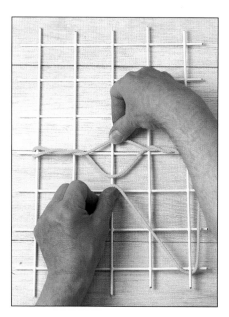

5 Lead the line down and around a corner lashing, then back to tuck centrally through the nearest centre side of the twisted portion of the lashing.

6 Take the line down around the next corner anchorage point.

7 Then bring it up through the central diamond that gives this hitch its distinctive name.

8 Take the line around the third anchorage point and bring it back to tuck once more through the central diamond shape.

9 Lead the line around the remaining corner anchorage, and then bring it back down to the starting point. Secure it at this point.

Trucker's Hitch

Still used by truck drivers to lash down loads securely – wherever rope lashings have not been superseded by webbing straps with mechanical tensioning and locking devices – this hitch can be traced back to the carters and hawkers who once went from house to house and town to town on horse-drawn conveyances. In those days it was known as the waggoner's hitch, but its application has changed little since then.

1 Attach the lashing to an anchorage point on the far side of the vehicle or trailer, then bring it over the load to the nearside.

2 Cast an anticlockwise (counter-clockwise) overhand loop in the line or lashing.

3 Make a bight in the standing part of the line and tuck it up (from the back to the front) through the pre-formed loop.

4 Impart an anticlockwise (counterclockwise) half twist to the long loop resulting from the tucked bight.

5 Add an extra half twist, creating a pair of interlocked elbows in the long lower loop.

6 Pull another bight from the standing part, this time bringing it through the twisted lower loop.

7 Pass the latest lower loop over an anchorage point on the nearside of the vehicle.

8 Take the line along and lead it around another anchorage on the same side of the vehicle; then toss it over the load to the far side. Repeat steps 2–7 as often as necessary to secure the load.

Round Mat

This knotted roundel can replace an ordinary mat, or it may be glued as ornamentation or embellishment to items as diverse as a collage picture or a drum majorette's uniform.

1 Middle a length of cord and cast an anticlockwise (counterclockwise) overhand loop in the working end.

2 Bring the working end down behind the loop and arrange a symmetrical pretzel layout.

3 Pick up the other end of the cord and tuck it diagonally (up and to the left) over/under/over.

4 Lead the working end around clockwise and tuck diagonally (down and to the right) under/over/under/over.

5 Tuck the end alongside the standing part. Follow the original lead around to double or triple the knot ply. Glue or stitch the end in place on the underside.

Carrick Mat

This can be used as an actual mat, or as a component of other art and craft work. Made around the hand, the same knot can form a necktie ring.

1 Cast a clockwise overhand loop in a length of cord or rope.

2 Bring the working end down over the original loop and arrange a pretzel layout.

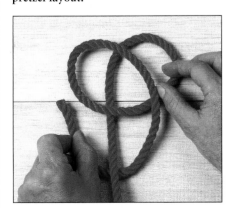

3 Pass the working end around (from right to left), keeping it behind the standing part.

4 Tuck it clockwise around and through the knot going over/under/over/under.

5 Tuck the working end alongside and parallel to the standing part. Follow the original lead around to double or triple the knot ply.

227

Ocean Plait

This good-looking design can be executed in the finest twines or the thickest ropes. Consequently it may be used as a table mat or coaster, an embellishment for bandsmen and women's uniforms, a doormat, or you might frame one and hang it on the wall.

Pin thicker materials on to a cork board or polystyrene tile to keep them in place until you have made the final locking tuck.

1 Cast an anticlockwise (counterclockwise) overhand loop in it with one end of a fairly long length of line.

2 Bend the long working end around (to the left) and lay it over the standing end of the original loop.

3 Take the end up and lay it (from left to right) over the top loop.

4 Lead the working end diagonally down (from right to left) and lay it on top of the lower loop.

5 Pick up the other half of the line – which now becomes the working end – and lay it (from left to right) over the new standing part.

6 Tuck the end diagonally (up and to the right), under/under, through the nearest loop.

7 Bring the working end around and take it diagonally from right to left over/under/over/under the knot parts.

8 Tuck the working end diagonally again (this time up from left to right), going over/under/over/under/over so that it comes out at the bottom right.

9 Tuck the working end up alongside the standing part, following the original lead around to double or triple the knot.

Long Mat

The traditional name for this is a prolong knot because the length of the mat can be extended. Given enough material (and patience), it would be possible to continue adding indefinitely to this knot. More realistically, it is used when an ocean plait is not quite long enough and needs to be enlarged.

1 Middle – more or less – a length of cord suitable for the use to which the finished mat will be put.

2 Cast a clockwise overhand loop and bring the working end around to create a long lefthand bight.

3 Lay the long working end (from left to right) over the upper bight.

4 Taking the standing part, make a long righthand bight, on top of the previous working end, to match the lefthand bight.

5 Tuck the working end diagonally down (from right to left), over/over/under, and lay it on top of the long lefthand bight.

6 Impart a clockwise lefthand twist to the lefthand bight.

7 Impart a similar clockwise twist to the righthand long bight.

8 Lay the twisted righthand bight over the top of the twisted lefthand bight.

9 Tuck the lefthand working end diagonally (down from left to right), under/over/over/under.

10 Tuck the righthand working end diagonally (down from right to left), over/under/over/under/over.

11 Arrange the interwoven mat layout symmetrically and remove unwanted slack. Tuck the working end alongside the standing part and follow around the original lead to double or triple the mat.

Alternate Ring Hitching

Large metal rings may be hitched over to prevent them banging and clanging against hard surfaces. Smaller ones make decorative finger-holds for blind pulls, etc. Needleworkers with stamina may make dozens or hundreds of very fine ones and then stitch them together to produce lace or tatted-like wall hangings or quilts.

1 Thread a length of cord and thread it on to the ring to be covered.

2 Tie a reversed pair of half hitches, resembling a bale sling hitch.

3 Add a third half hitch, which must be the mirror-image of the second one, and pulled tight up against it.

4 Add a fourth half hitch, which must be the mirror-image of the third, and therefore the same as the second.

5 Repeat steps 2 to 4 as often as required to cover the ring completely with the cord.

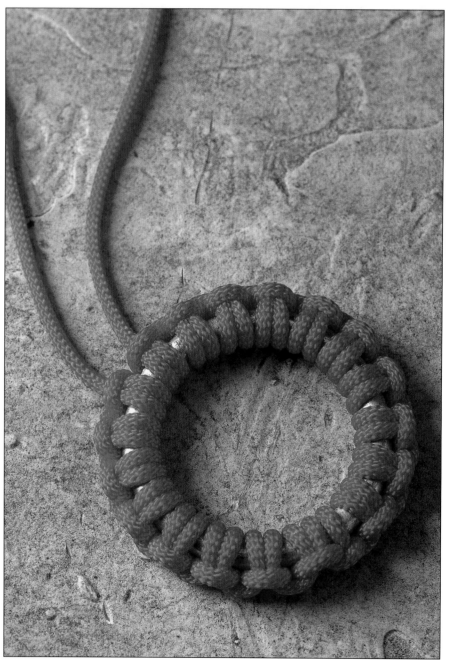

Endless Double Chain

Join the ends of a double chain to make a handsome body ornament or incorporate it into art and craft work. While the steps are illustrated in two different colours, for clarity, this chain is more usually made with the two ends of a single cord.

1 Bring the standing and working ends of a double chain close together.

2 Pass the working end up (from back to front) through the final loop of the standing end.

3 Tuck the end up through the knot parts beside itself (from back to front).

4 Tuck the working end down (from front to back), under one knot part, through the loop.

5 Tuck the end sideways (from top to bottom of the illustration), going over/under/over/over, as it picks up the second loop in from the standing end.

6 Lead the working end up (from back to front), going under/under, bringing it up to emerge from the third of the working end loops.

7 Finally, tuck the end down (from front to back), over/under/under, to meet up with the standing part of the line.

241

Braid Knot

It is possible, using this single-strand knot, to replicate the familiar three-strand pigtail plait (braid); which can then be employed to shorten rope or cord, or to decorate it. The braid knot also makes a practical makeshift handle for a suitcase or sailing dinghy daggerplate.

1 Cast a long clockwise underhand loop, with three parallel cord parts.

2 Begin the plait (braid) by bringing the righthand strand over the middle strand, to lie inside and below the lefthand strand.

3 Then take the lefthand strand over the middle strand, to lie inside and below the righthand strand.

4 Repeat step 2, noting how the outermost (furthest away) strand becomes the working one each time.

5 Repeat step 3, complying once more with the principle that the least used strand becomes the next working one.

6 Continue plaiting alternate right and lefthand strands, pulling each step tight as the work develops.

MAKE FAST To attach a line to an anchorage or belay (often with a hitch).

MESSENGER The name for a throwing or heaving line when it is used to pull a thicker cord or rope across an intervening space.

MIDDLE Used as a verb, to double a rope or cord so as to locate its centre.

MONOFILAMENT Continuous synthetic fibre of uniform diameter and circular cross-section larger than 50 micons/$\frac{1}{500}$ in. (See also Multifilament.)

MULTIFILAMENT Very fine continuous synthetic fibre of uniform diameter and circular cross section less than 50 microns/$\frac{1}{500}$ in. (See also Monofilament.)

NATURAL FIBRE Processed plant products used to make rope and other cordage.

NIP The point within a knot where friction may be concentrated.

NOOSE A free-running, sliding or adjustable loop.

NYLON The first synthetic (manmade) fibre of merit available to the cordage industry. There are two grades: Nylon 66 is extensively used in the UK and USA; Nylon 6 (made available under trade names such as Perlon and Enkalon) is widely used in Europe and Japan, as well as being available in the UK and USA.

OVERHAND LOOP A loop (clockwise or anticlockwise/counterclockwise) in which the working end is laid on top of the standing part. (See also Loop.)

PLAIT A term generally interchangeable with braid, but which can refer only to interwoven strands forming a pattern that is three-dimensional in cross-section. (See also Braid.)

POLYESTER A widely used synthetic cordage (trade names Dacron and Terylene).

POLYETHYLENE A polyolefin synthetic (manmade) fibre (commonly known as Polythene/plastic).

POLYPROPYLENE A versatile polyolefin synthetic fibre.

PRUSIKING To climb a rope using a knot that jams when downward pressure is applied but can slide up the rope when the weight is removed.

RAPPEL See Abseil.

REEF Boating – to reduce sail area in strong winds (verb); each individual fold or roll of sail taken in (noun).

ROPE Cordage over 10 mm/$\frac{5}{12}$ in in diameter.

ROUND TURN In which a working end completely encircles a ring, rail, post or rope, and finishes up alongside its own standing part. (See also Turn.)

S-LAID Lefthanded (anticlockwise/counterclockwise).

SAFE WORKING LOAD The estimated load a rope may withstand, taking into account various weakening factors (wear and tear, damage, effect of knots and other uses); it may be as little as one-seventh the quoted breaking strength. (See Breaking Strength.)

SECURITY The integral stability of a knot.

SLING An endless rope or webbing (tape) band or strop.

SMALL STUFF A casual term for any cordage, not rope.

SOFT LAID Any flexible rope and cordage.

SPLIT FILM Synthetic (manmade), ribbon-like fibres produced from a plastic sheet.

STANDING END The inactive end of cord. (See also Working End.)

STANDING PART That part of a rope or cord anywhere between working and standing ends.

STAPLE FIBRES Graded natural fibres of limited length and strength, due to their plant origins; also discontinuous synthetic (manmade) fibres created by cutting filaments into discrete lengths.

STRAND The largest element of a rope, made from contra-twisted yarns.

STRENGTH The integral ability of knotted cordage to withstand a load.

STRING Relatively cheap and disposable small cord and twine.

STROP See Sling.

SYNTHETIC ROPE Cordage that is made from synthetic (manmade) multifilaments, monofilaments, staple fibres or split film.

TAG END Angling – working end.

THIMBLE A metal or plastic lining for an eye.

THREAD Fine line.

TURN A 360 degree wrap around a rig, rail, post or rope. (See also Round Turn.)

UNDERHAND LOOP A loop in which the working end is laid beneath the standing part.

WHIPPING A binding to prevent a rope's end from fraying.

WORKING END The active end of a rope or cord. (See also Standing End.)

YARN The basic element of rope strands, spun from natural fibres or synthetic (manmade) materials.

Z-LAID Righthanded (clockwise).

Index

Further Information

SUPPLIERS

English Braids, Spring Lane, Malvern WR14 1AL
Tel: 01684 892 222
Fax: 01684 892 111
Their marine sales division caters for the recreational sector and sail boat racing. Suppliers of barrier ropes, starter cords, shock cords, whipping twines, webbing and web-lash securing systems, and stainless steel hollow fids. Contact them for the location of your nearest stockist.

Eurorope Limited, 4 Phoenix Court, Atkinson Way, Foxhills Industrial Estate, Scunthorpe DN15 8QJ
Tel: 01724 280 480
Fax: 01724 857 750
Wholesale suppliers of rope, cord, twines, nets, lifting gear slings and accessories. Contact them for the location of your nearest stockist.

Des & Liz Pawson, Footrope Knots, 501 Wherstead Road, Ipswich, Suffolk IP2 8LL
Tel: 01473 690 090
Suppliers of traditional rope, cordage and smaller stuff; wire rope and chain; canvas; tools; fittings; fenders, knotboards, chest beckets and other knotwork; books (new, secondhand and rare). Their unique ropework museum may be visited free (by prior arrangement).

Kevin Keatley, K.J.K. Ropeworks, Town Living Farmhouse, Puddington, Tiverton, Devon EX16 8LW
Tel/fax: 01884 860 692
Supplier of cords and fittings, especially braided synthetics. Price list on request.

Leanda, 39 Borrowdale Drive, Norwich, Norfolk NR1 4LY
Tel/fax: 01603 434 707
Textile craft equipment manufacturers; specialists in Japanese-style braiding and passementerie equipment; accessories for spinning and weaving; also a book list.

Marlow Ropes Ltd, Diplocks Way, Hailsham, East Sussex BN27 3JS
Tel: 01323 847 234
Fax: 01323 440 093
email: yachting@marlow ropes.com
Website: http://www.marlow ropes.com
Market leaders in yacht rope technology and such accessories as shockcord, barrier ropes, toestrap and buoyancy bag webbing, whipping twine, splicing kits, sail repair tapes.

Ann Norman, Sagaman, Aston Road, Bampton, Oxfordshire, OX18 2AL
Tel/fax: 01993 850 823
email: sagaman@compuserve.com
Designer, handweaver and maker of cords, including four-strand cords, and ropes of traditional laid structure. Advice offered and commissions accepted.

Oakhurst Quality Products Limited, Warsop Trading Estate, Hever Road, Edenbridge, Kent TN8 5LD
Tel: 01732 866 668
Fax: 01732 864 555
Wholesale suppliers of rope, twine, cordage, chain, doormats, work gloves, garden sundries. Contact Brenda Risdon for the location of your nearest stockist.

BIBLIOGRAPHY

Asher, Harry, *The Alternative Knot Book* (Nautical Books, A. & C. Black, London, 1989)
Ashley, Clifford Warren, *The Book of Knots* (Doubleday, New York, 1944/Faber & Faber, London, 1947)
Bailey, Hazel, *Knotting for Guides* (Girl Guides Association, London, 1987)
Chisnall, Robert (Editor), *Rock Climbing Safety Manual* (Ontario Rock Climbing Association, Canada, 1984)
Day, Cyrus Lawrence, *Quipus & Witches' Knots* (University of Kansas Press, 1967)
Graumont, Raoul, and Hensel, John, *The Encyclopaedia of Knots and Fancy Rope Work* (Cornell Maritime Press, Cambridge, Maryland, 1939)
Graves, Richard H., *The Bushcraft Handbooks* (Graves, Sydney, 1952)
Griend, P. van de, and Turner, J.C. (eds), *The History and Science of Knots* (World Scientific Publishing Company, Singapore, New Jersey, London, Hong Kong, 1996)
I.G.K.T., *Knotting Matters* (1982 to the present)
Kreh, Lefty, and Sosin, Mark, *Practical Fishing & Boating Knots* (A. & C. Black, London, 1975)
Luebben, Craig, *Knots for Climbers* (Chockstone Press, Evergreen, Colorado, 1993)
March, Bill, *Mountain Rope Techniques* (Cicerone Press, Cumbria, 1983)
Noonan, Michael, *Climbing Knots – for Lefties and Righties* (I.C.S. Books, Merryville, Indiana, 1997)
Padgett, Allen, & Smith, Bruce, *On Rope* (National Speleological Society, Huntsville, Alabama, 1992)
Payne, Lee and Bob, "The Forgotten Zeppelin Knot" (*Boating Magazine*, March 1976)
Perkins, Andy, Tapes, *Slings & Harnesses* (Troll Safety Equipment, 1991)
Rosenow, Frank, *Seagoing Knots* (W.W. Norton, New York, 1990)
Shaw, George Russell, *Knots – Useful & Ornamental* (Bonanza Books, New York, 1924 and 1933)
Spencer, Charles L., *Knots, Splices & Fancy Work* (Brown, Son & Fergusson, Glasgow, 1934)
Sweet, John, *Scout Pioneering* (Scout Association, London, 1974)
Toss, Brion, *The Rigger's Apprentice* International Marine Publishing Co, Camden, Maine, 1984)
Trower, Nola, *Knots and Ropework* (Helmsman Books, Marlborough, Wiltshire, 1992)
Vare, Alan B., *The Hardy Book of Fisherman's Knots* (Camden Publishing, London, 1987)
Warner, Charles, *A Fresh Approach to Knotting and Ropework* (Warner, Yanderra, NSW, 1992)

ACKNOWLEDGEMENTS

The author is indebted to David Ierston, marine sales manager for English Braids Ltd, who supplied superb cordage for this book.

The following, from whom the cordage was obtained to tie most of the specimen knots illustrated, were also generous with their time and advice: Brenda Risdon (Oakhurst Quality Products Ltd.); Kevin Keatley (K.J.K. Ropeworks); James Martin (Marlow Ropes Ltd.); Des & Liz Pawson (Footrope Knots).

A special extra acknowledgement is due to Des Pawson who, by allowing access to his home and workplace, made possible the unique portraits of traditional ropework that enrich this book.

ORGANIZATIONS

The International Guild of Knot Tyers was established in 1982 and now has a worldwide membership. It is a registered educational charity, dedicated to preserving and promoting the art, craft and science of knots.

Anyone – expert or novice – interested in tying knots may join. IGKT members enjoy a quarterly magazine, *Knotting Matters,* in addition to regular meetings. For more details and an application form, contact:

Nigel Harding,
IGKT Honorary Secretary,
16 Egles Grove, Uckfield, East Sussex TN22 2BY, England
Tel: 01825 760 425
e-mail:
igkt@nigelharding.demon.uk
(Knotting can also be found on the Internet.)